CHAIRS
IN COLOUR

John Chelfey

CHAIR & CABINET MAKER

At the Hand & Chair

The *first Shop from Ludgate Street*

in S.t Pauls Church Ya.d

Makes & Sells all sorts of

chairs & Cabinets

Chairs in Colour

LANTO SYNGE

BLANDFORD PRESS
Poole   ·   Dorset

First published in 1978
by Blandford Press Ltd,
Link House, West Street, Poole,
Dorset BH15 1LL

Copyright © Lanto Synge 1978

ISBN 0 7137 0828 X

Colour printed by Sackville Press, Billericay

Text printed in Great Britain by
Fletcher & Son Ltd, Norwich and bound by
Richard Clay (The Chaucer Press) Ltd,
Bungay, Suffolk

Contents

Acknowledgements

I am grateful to Mallett and Son for providing many of the photographs reproduced in this book and for much other kind assistance. Other photographs have been made available by the Dean and Chapter of Westminster, George Rainbird Ltd., and the Victoria and Albert Museum London. The photographs of the furniture from the tomb of Tutankhamun were taken by F. L. Kenett, other photographs were specially taken by Bob Loosemore.

I love it I love it, and who shall dare
  To chide me for loving that old arm chair,
I've treasured it long as a holy prize,
  I've bedew'd it with tears, and embalm'd it with sighs;
'Tis bound by a thousand bands to my heart;
  Not a tie will break it, not a link will start.
Would ye learn the spell, a mother sat there,
  And a sacred thing is that old arm chair.
                    The Old Arm Chair, Eliza Cook 1836

1

Early Ceremonial and Other Origins

The barge she sat in, like a burnished throne
Burn'd on the water; . . .
                                            . . . and Anthony,
Enthron'd i' the market-place, did sit alone,
Whistling to the air . . .

I have no hestiation in beginning with the origin of chairs and in making some observations concerning the history of the form, especially since the modern styles have constantly referred back in design to ideas, or elements of design, or details of ornament, from earlier times. No type is too early to have been reflected to a greater or lesser extent in later models, nor any primitive form too basic or too simple to have had influence on modern standards.

The first and foremost influences in the style of the chair form have, of course, from the very beginning been dictated by the construction of the seat. That is, the very fact that if it is made of planks or slats of stone put together in box-like form it has one type of appearance; if it is made of crossed timber in X-shape form it has another; or if it is of a softer, pliable substance such as wickerwork or skins it has a different one again. These basic variations naturally reveal overriding aspects of construction which would seem to be totally independent. But even these classic structures could be combined in the development of a piece of furniture for better support and comfort. In turn the form became in Europe more and more complex in the pursuit of such qualities and also, perhaps even more significantly, in the pursuit of an impressive style for ceremonial display, and this later merged into refined elegance.

The basic forms evolved quickly to highly sophisticated and decorative semi-art objects, the epitome of which were produced in the eighteenth and nineteenth centuries. It is these and the fine chairs of the preceding century or so that are the chief focus of study in this book. The actual construction of such pieces became extremely involved and a note on the technicalities of this subject is included later in the text.

However, I must first be allowed, before further digression, to mention some of the touchstones of earlier chair history, which have to greater and lesser extents, consciously and unconsciously, influenced later makers and even some of the great fashioners of the furniture designs of the eighteenth and nineteenth centuries. A knowledge of the existence of some of the primitive, naive and original specimens enriches one's appreciation of the masterpieces of cabinet-making and chair-making of other ages and cultures, not always as remote as one might imagine. An awareness for cross-reference and comparison can help us to evaluate the qualities of individual examples of any time or origin, and heightens our delight in the sophisticated masterpieces of eighteenth-century Europe.

Words and Historic Connotations

In the English language the very word chair has a wide variety of nuances and a glance at a dictionary immediately brings to mind a kaleidoscope of ideas from qualifications such as armchair, bathchair, deckchair, easy chair, etc. or the historic sedan chair and the macabre electric chair to meanings connected with the user of this specific type of furniture. The word itself is thought to have derived via Middle English, Old French and Latin from the Greek 'kathedra' from which is, of course, also directly adopted the word 'cathedral', the church where a bishop has his throne. This is the centre point from which his authority extends and in a similar context an announcement made 'Ex Cathedra' is one which is understood to be official and authoritative. The bishop's throne is considered to be a highly important focal point in the ritual of his religious duties, being a symbol of authority and spiritual rank. Many old cathedrals have fine examples, often huge edifices of stone, wood or a combination of the two. They are normally placed between the choir stalls and the high altar at the east end of the building.

Originally, in most Christian churches, the Jewish and Roman system was adopted: a throne would be placed in the centre of an apse at the east end of the church. A most interesting relic of this custom is to be seen at Norwich Cathedral in England. The bishop's throne there is elevated behind the high altar and facing westwards down the choir and nave. Dating from about the eighth century, and originally elaborately carved in wood, only the nucleus now remains in a much altered state, remembering that the cathedral itself has been rebuilt several times since its origin. However, it is an interesting survival of a once much practised habit, originally inspired one supposes by the Biblical reference:

'I was in the Spirit, and behold, a throne . . .'

Canon Thurlow records fifth-century documentation of such a throne:

'Let there be a throne towards the east . . . let the place of the throne be raised three steps for the Altar ought also to be there.'

Mediaeval thrones survive elsewhere, for example the stone throne of St Thomas à Becket which stands at the east end of Canterbury Cathedral. A magnificent example of a mediaeval carved wood throne in the Gothic style is in Exeter Cathedral. Amongst the decoration of the pinnacles high above the Bishop's seat is a carved wood mitre. This throne was carefully dismantled during the last world war and stored away safely in case the Cathedral should have suffered damage; it was subsequently reconstructed in its original place.

Less huge but perhaps of greater ceremonial importance are the thrones of kingship. Again, these are the very symbol of authority and power, so much so that the beginning of a reign is marked by the fact that the monarch 'came to the throne' at a certain time. The abstract term 'the throne' meaning essentially the monarchy has the key understanding so often attributed to terms connected with types of seat furniture, i.e. an indication of important status. 'The throne' is almost synonymous with 'the crown' in the symbolism of state. In accordance with this, the King's actual throne is often made in a suitably grand and noble manner and frequently takes on historic connections itself. In England, the throne known as the Coronation Chair, permanently preserved in Westminster Abbey, is a superb object enshrouded by a mass of interesting legend and historical background. It is in this chair that the Sovereign is crowned, a tradition dating back over many hundreds of years. The woodwork of the chair itself is of the fourteenth century, of decorated Gothic architectural form in oak and bearing traces of original painting and gilding. Originally it must have been brightly coloured but it now has a delightful mellowed texture. The lion feet are an eighteenth-century restoration. Perhaps the most fascinating part of this great throne is the Stone of Scone which is enclosed beneath the woodwork of the seat. This ancient lump of rock was brought to Westminster by Edward the Confessor, as an already ancient and famed seat of kingship. It originated in Ireland as the Celtic 'Lia Fail' erected in Icolmkil for the coronation of Fergus Eric. His son is said to have led the Dalriads to the shores of Argyllshire and brought the stone with him. At Scone in Fife it became the coronation chair of Scotland and remained there until Edward I removed it and enclosed it within his coronation chair in Westminster Abbey.

Other than the Coronation Chair there are thrones of different ages in various ceremonial chambers of the United Kingdom. The most important of these is the splendid throne at the centre of Parliament in the Palace of Westminster. Dominating as it does the House of Lords, it is complete in its setting with a canopy above it and flanked by metal candelabra. Here we have a sign of a full turn of history and design, for it is a nineteenth-century revival of what is the essence of the Coronation Chair – high Gothic splendour, architectural again but this time the calculated synthesis of the ideals and delights of Barry and Pugin, the great Victorian designers of the Houses of Parliament. Made in about 1830 it is made of oak richly carved with the Royal Arms on the back, these being painted and gilded. From this centre-point of government and legislation the Queen proclaims solemnly the chief pronouncements of the government. The ritual is still there even if the words, known to be the thoughts of ministers, are not now always accepted as 'ex cathedra'.

Within parliament we note that government jurisdiction in England is presided over by the Lord Chancellor, who since the reign of Elizabeth I has taken his seat on a woolsack; sessions or sittings depend on its being occupied. The House of Lords meetings begin and end with the arrival and departure of the Chancellor:

The Lord Chancellor took his seat upon the woolsack . . .

is reported in the daily papers and parliamentary records. The Speaker of the House of Commons, the other debating chamber, is the only person in the chamber to sit on a chair; the other members, even the Prime Minister and Cabinet sit on benches on either side of the house. However, Members of Parliament are elected to 'seats' from every part of the country and, as such, each is put in a position of authority on behalf of his constituency. In some places a successful candidate was 'chaired' by his electorate and paraded in an elaborate seat around the town. A curious surviving chair of this type can be seen in Norwich museum in England. This ancient custom is still practised widely in many countries. The Pope is from time to time borne through his congregation in a chair or litter, or similarly victorious sportsmen are 'chaired' at the spur of the moment on the games field, being mounted on their team's shoulders. In the same context as a Member of Parliament's seat must be mentioned, the use of the word as referring to a residence, usually the country residence of a gentleman, whose 'seat' or seats are at the centre of his landed property, an aspect carried over from feudal days.

Over and over again the language reveals the importance of chairs and the different words describing individual types are an indication of the variety of uses with which they are connected. Uniting all these is the conception of the superiority and authority which the occupant held, and the necessity of having some person in such a position.

> '*Is the chair empty? is the sword unsway'd?*
> *Is the King dead? the empire unpossess'd?*'

Shakespeare's words from Richard III carry this essential belief as a necessity for efficient political calm. A throne or chair was always a symbol of high status; the fact that a leader was placed in it meant that he had assumed a place of authority and signified his attention to high duty and his intention of supervising whatever proceedings were going on. University professors are said to have 'chairs' in subjects of which they are the official exponents and teachers.

The term 'chairman' as of a business or any other meeting is derived from the same tradition and the 'chairmanship' is a position of leadership. In this case, as in the use of the word 'board', meaning table in the strict sense of the word but otherwise a group of leaders (e.g. Board of Directors), the function of furniture as a privileged commodity signifies a status symbol.

The Earliest Chairs

The ebb and flow of civilisations has over the centuries created and buried all manner of fine and sophisticated furniture including chairs. How fantastic are those perfect furniture fossils discovered in Egypt in 1922 hidden since 1350 BC from human eyes. Tutankhamun's throne together with other furniture discovered in his tomb displays an extraordinary richness of technical mastery in woodwork, inlay, gilding and general cabinet-making. This art was lost for over two and a half thousand years before it was equalled in Europe. The Pharaoh's throne is a design of wood covered in embossed gold and silver and inlaid with semi-precious stones. The monopoid legs and the leopard or lion masks are decorative forms which were revived again in early nineteenth-century French and English furniture. A foot stool, also from the tomb, used by the boy-king at the beginning of his reign has the same fascinating modern look and paw feet; these paws face one direction (as on an animal!) and not outwards as on a Chippendale stool. The other masterpiece relevant in this context is the great throne which again has a large 'sling' seat, no arms, but X-frame legs and an upright back. Unlike the stool it is not chiefly of embossed metal but is profusely decorated with inlaid materials. The richness of this and the gold throne are breathtaking and each remarkable for its sculptural quality; one seems a foretaste of the finest of Regency creations while the other has an appearance that is wholly contemporary in shape.

The above is brief mention of a few aspects of the earliest ceremonial uses of chairs as reflected by some remaining specimens and as suggested by word usage. No item of furniture has been of greater cultural importance or indicated more aspects of our changing rituals, habits and life-styles. It is curious and significant that even today armchairs are placed at the ends of a dining table for the head of a household or hosts at a party. This tradition must have re-emerged after the introduction of long dining tables in England towards the end of the eighteenth century.

2 *Middle Ages and Post Mediaeval*

If you please to take the privilege o' sitting down.

A visit to a picture gallery will instantly give some impression of the nature of mediaeval and other early chairs, and indeed often of later models as well. The fine Gothic painters of Europe and their successors have depicted an interesting variety of thrones and stately chairs, especially in the much-favoured religious groups depicting, for example, the Virgin Mary seated on a throne and holding the infant Christ. Sometimes only a hint is given of the nature of the Madonna's seat, but on other occasions paintings and sculptural reliefs of the subject, or even architectural decoration as, for example, on the walls and portals of great cathedrals, give a clearer view. It is true, of course, that the types of throne or chair depicted may be wholly conjecture of an historic type on the part of the painter or sculptor, but usually we can assume that the throne and other furnishings are largely based on reasonable evidence or, at any rate, reflect types known and used at the time of the execution of the work. Manuscripts likewise depict, in detailed illuminations, furniture that can not have been created totally from the imagination of the monks who made them. These certainly give clues about the earliest forms, so few of which have survived due to their perishable nature. A psalter made in Canterbury about 1147, now at Trinity College, Cambridge, for example, contains a large illustration of Eadwine, the scribe, who wrote this famous manuscript, seated in profile on a chair. He is working with both hands at a book which rests on a partly covered desk. Both the chair and the

The Coronation Chair.

17

desk are of Romanesque form; the chair has a low back and arms, only just higher than the seat, and in shape is largely architectural with the corner supports looking like thin columns and the side panel of the piece being decorated with three series of rounded arches, the middle row plain and elongated.

Many of the earliest European seats were exclusively ceremonial, either related to the court or to the church, and are essentially architectural in form. This is borne out both by the few surviving examples like the Coronation Chair and by representations in the decorative arts. Thrones were only made for important use and ceremonial places and it is not surprising that they should be created in the manner of, and to fit in with, fine architectural settings; they were characteristically in keeping with the nature of their surroundings. The legacy of such an obvious and commonsense unity of style persisted through the centuries: ideally, a chair designed by Robert Adam to take an example from the zenith of furniture design was made to correspond closely with the room in which it was to be placed.

But to revert to Eadwine the scribe, it is particularly interesting to note that his chair is elaborately painted with bright colours – red, blue, green and gold. It is not the dark brown polished oak we might otherwise have assumed. Like the Coronation Chair which still has traces of paint on it, most mediaeval furniture was highly decorated, as was no doubt much of the other woodwork of the great churches. The rows of choir stalls, now a familiar and lovely polished dark brown were probably more like the nineteenth-century restored stalls in the choir at Westminster Abbey. Bright colours played an important part in the presentation of splendour and pomp that accompanied the prominence of courtly and episcopal life. Other trappings included (as paintings and manuscripts again show) costly and rich-looking fabrics; thrones were frequently placed under a fabric canopy with a panel of the same textile hung behind the seat. A fifteenth-century miniature in Froissart's Chronicles, at the Bibliothèque Nationale, Paris, depicts Gregory XI seated in a wooden chair over which hangs a canopy and backing of precious cloth. Similarly, a painting by F. Surbaran in Seville shows Pope Urban II giving an audience to a saint: the Pope is seated on a fairly plain chair beneath an elaborate, quite separate, canopy fringed with tassels, while the saint is placed on a mere box-like stool with an upholstered top and with no canopy. With the greater availability of fine materials lavish uses were made of them as we shall shortly see.

Very few chairs from the middle ages have survived. On the whole it is the larger, stronger and more heavily made throne type, especially those made for churches, that remain as representatives of the times. An oak chair at St Mary's Church, Little Dunmow, Essex dates from the middle of the thirteenth century – it is probably somewhat altered from its original appearance and was probably part of a series of seats but it retains much of the character of the age. The seat is of panelled-in box form and the curved arms are panelled to the base of the chair. The sides of the seat are decorated with Gothic tracery and roundels. The low back is decorated on the inside with three small Gothic trefoil arches. Another much later English Gothic survivor is the very fine chair of the Master of the United Guild of St Mary, St John and St Catherine at Coventry. This solid piece of furniture which would have been placed on a dais, is magnificently decorated with elaborate high Gothic tracery and is topped with large finials in the form of carved animals. In a painting in Westminster Abbey Richard II is shown seated on a similar chair (see PLATE 1).

Fewer still of the domestic chairs which were made on a lighter scale have survived. Chairs in houses were not at all common; only the master and perhaps the mistress of the household had one. Other people would sit on benches and stools as a matter of course. Another reason for the few surviving examples is the fact that most domestic furniture was of a light portable nature and was therefore far more fragile than the solid church pieces which remained *in situ*. Much mediaeval furniture was carried about regularly, as is indicated by the use of the continental words suggesting 'movables': meubles, mueblos, mobilia, möbeln, meubelen, etc. Even chairs of state would be carried about as suggested by the Ewelme Inventory of 1466 which lists the Duke of Suffolk's 'chaire of tymbre of astate' with 'a case of lether thereto' into which it was packed.

To be portable some chairs were made in the old Greek and

Roman form in folding **X** fashion. A fine and interesting survivor of this type is the folding seat from Styria in the Oesterreichisches Museum für Angewandte Kunst, Vienna. This Celtic looking piece which dates from as early as 1200 or thereabouts, is carved with animal heads at the feet and on the four top corners, and intricate relief decoration on the other surfaces. The actual seat across the **X**-frame was of leather. This style of crossed timber structure was to remain in favour for centuries throughout Europe. The form was particularly associated with a more comfortable type of padded chair that evolved with the increased availability and new use of fabrics such as velvet and silk, which were imported to many countries from or through Italy. There is a sixteenth-century **X**-shaped chair at Winchester Cathedral that was originally elaborately padded with upholstery and covered with blue velvet, fastened down with big-headed gilt nails. The chair is said to have been used by Queen Mary at her marriage to Philip of Spain in 1554. Of the same type is the well-preserved chair and footstool which belonged to Archbishop Juxon, in the Victoria and Albert Museum, London. This wide chair still looks as soft and inviting as it always did and is exemplary of the search for comfort that was sought around the beginning of the seventeenth century. Less comforting is the thought that Charles I, a great patron of the arts, is said to have used it at his trial, moments before his execution. For luxurious covering, however, that chair is exceeded by some of the wonderful original furnishings of Knole Park, Kent. These include a very similar chair, astonishingly well preserved, upholstered and covered with an appliqué of cloth of gold on a ground of red satin. Other rich and comfortable chairs are recorded in the Lumley Castle inventory of 1609 which lists:

> 'chaires of cloth of gold and silver'
> 'purple cloth of gold chayre'
> 'needle work chaires'
> 'chaires of crimson silk'
> 'purple velvett chaires'
> and similar 'quishions'

Turkey work was also used as a covering; this was a fabric with a knotted texture and patterns resembling oriental carpets. Luxurious chairs such as these seem totally unrelated to the prosaic hard wooden furniture that was produced for other circumstances.

Oak chair, covered with Turkey-work. Mid-17th-century.

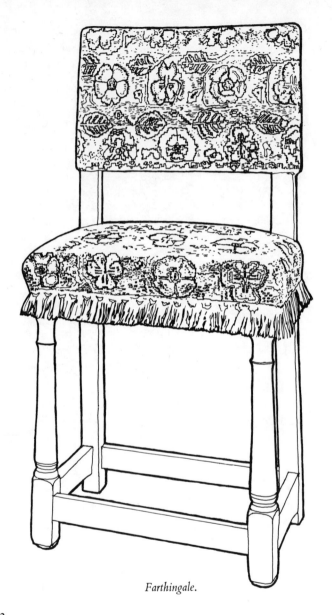

Farthingale.

Oak chair, carved and inlaid. About 1600.

Wooden chairs were made of any timber that was available – oak predominantly, but also elm, ash, beech, fruitwood, mulberry and yew. Sometimes these woods were inlaid into each other while holly, ebony and stained woods would be used for fairly crude early marquetry. Other than this, carving was used decoratively in the form of strapwork, bearing a resemblance to elements in the Tudor decorative plasterwork on ceilings, or as in the woodwork of larger form such as the panelled 'screens', the bottom end wall of the main dining hall of a great house, college or institution. A further popular enrichment was split bobbin-work. This consisted of applied rows of half balls of wood, having first been made in complete form by turning on a lathe and then halved. This method of workmanship was used widely for more than merely decorative features. Chairs were made of entirely turned members and are frequently referred to as 'thrown' chairs. Made exclusively by turners using chisels and lathes they produced a bobbin or spindle effect that was popular well into the seventeenth century. In America, turning remained in vogue for considerably longer. A curious English product of this type of work was the triangular-seated bobbin chair, such as the one illustrated (PLATE 5). This rather shapeless and undoubtedly uncomfortable specimen is entirely composed of many dozens of turned pieces around the solitary flat section that forms the seat. Such chairs are thought by some to be an archaic type from Scandinavia and probably of Byzantine origin.

Chairs were made by a variety of craftsmen, including coffre-makers and joiners. The latter became more and more important in the art of chair-making towards the end of the fifteenth century producing pieces consisting of frames containing panels. The panels might be decorated with linenfold carving on the outside of the box-like structure, but the frame itself was fixed together with mortise and tenon joints, that is, tongue in slot joints not visible from the exterior of the woodwork. This was the basis of the true art of chair-making and still remains so, for it is always essential that for wear chairs must be firm and strong, however lightly constructed. As the form and designs became more complex and elaborate the skill of the chair-maker became more specialised and independent. Much later on

Sheraton, in his *Cabinet Dictionary* of 1803 was to say of chair-making that it is

> 'generally confined to itself; as those who professedly work at it seldom engage to make cabinet furniture'.

The early joiners established themselves firmly in this art, and gave the name of their craft to 'joint' stools (joined stools). Of a plain simple form, these useful utilitarian objects consisted of a small rectangular seat supported by four slightly splayed-out legs, held together by plain stretchers. As well as for sitting on they were used for various purposes such as for resting a coffin on – according to earlier furniture history. Such stools were made from about the middle of the sixteenth century. A variant form of joint stool was the 'chaise de chant' on which a choir boy perched but would fall off should he doze off. From around this time also we note that the panelling was often omitted from between the framework of chairs, in such a way that, for example, the arms had an open space beneath them.

Other than the plainer functional chairs made during the age of oak we can note the emergence of more decorative styles. The effect of the Reformation in England largely coincided with the Italian Renaissance influence as it reached these out-lying parts of Europe; Henry VIII's rejection of the Pope was followed by an influx of both Protestant culture from the Low Countries and by scholastic ideas of style from Italy. An English oak armchair of the early seventeenth century in the Victoria and Albert Museum, London, not only has a back richly inlaid with various contrasting woods but the front legs are in the form of semi-classical fluted columns. At the same time we see the wholly secular nature of Dutch chairs and note the emergence of the 'farthingale', a simple chair with no arms, more like a stool with a back. This sort of light chair became highly popular all over Europe and could be supplied relatively easily in larger quantities. It had a simple domestic, practical appearance and lent itself to relatively unceremonial use.

Italian chairs and some English shell-back chairs display a more sculptural form that seems the antithesis of the farthingale. The shell-back form, indeed, owes much to the Italian spirit.

Many other variants were popular. The French caquetoire or conversation chair had a narrow upright back, often with carved decoration, slightly embracing, rounded arms, and simple legs and stretchers. This was adopted especially in Scotland. Yorkshire and Derbyshire varieties had their own characteristics, notably backs composed of hooped, arcaded rails. Another related item was the table chair, known in England as early as 1547 and popular throughout the seventeenth century. A fine example is the one at Cothele House, Devon which is dated 1627. This is an armchair with a wide tilting rectangular back that can be laid down over the arms and pinned in position to form a table.

Other relations in the chair family that should be borne in mind include such items as settles, log seats for three or more people, with arms at each end, and normally with high backs, and often with wings. Both of these features were for protection in houses that were far from draught-proof.

Of the age of oak we can generally conclude that chairs are conspicuously different from other pieces of furniture in their relative lightness of design and construction. From the Elizabethan age beds and cupboards were usually composed of massive timbers with huge bulb motifs and heavy carving, but seat furniture in contrast was made much more lightly. The farthingale chair was the ultimate development of this easy domestic simplicity.

3

New Kings, New Splendour

A Throne sent word to a Throne.

In France and England new kings emerged at almost simultaneous moments, bringing with them a vigour and boost to political and artistic achievements in, and radiating from, both nations.

The young Louis XIV, following the death of Cardinal Mazarin in 1661, began a fresh flourish of royal display and asserted himself fully through the prestige of the arts. Meanwhile in the previous year England saw the Restoration of its monarchy with the accession of Charles II, whose flamboyance came as a natural and splendid reaction following the dour and dull Puritanism that had triumphed since the Civil War. The French Court was much more ostentatious than the English. Versailles was the epitome of the Sun King's creations, and the furnishing of it was closely supervised under the King's excited and ambitious eye. He patronised new factories for the production of every variety of the decorative arts, and furniture was a principal ingredient of the rich interiors of the palace. Glorious cabinets of marquetry, lacquer or brass and tortoiseshell inlay in the manner of Boulle were made with beautifully chiselled and gilded bronze mounts (ormolu) fitted on to them for further enrichment. Understandably, major cabinets as these and other large items such as state beds and thrones, both with rich upholstery and hangings were the first and most important items to be supplied. On the whole, seat furniture was of less immediate necessity, the earlier types of chair being only slightly enriched, being basically of the same relatively straightforward practical nature that had been the norm during the previous half of the century. While the more prominent furniture made for the court (and similarly imitated to some extent by the nobility) was of the grandiose style and magnificent quality already cited, side tables and seating pieces were of carved wood either polished or for more important circumstances gilded. These pieces were themselves of fine quality and great beauty; the woodwork was sometimes elaborately carved with surface decoration in the form of light foliate strapwork interspersed with formal rosettes, scrolls and beading. But in chairs the simple scrolling lines of the legs and the neat and perfect mouldings of flatter parts such as stretchers persisted in an elegant form that must have been in some cases incongruous and in some cases a relief in contrast to the elaborate ostentation of important commodes made for the same rooms. Chairs such as these – there are fine examples in the Musée des Arts Décoratifs in Paris – were richly and comfortably upholstered. Costly fabrics, gilt fringes, and tassels, partly made up for the comparative simplicity of the woodwork, and were shown to their full on the high backs and fairly low wide seats. A little later a new richness of wood-carving decorated chairs in a new way with a foretaste of the baroque fantasies that were to come. Chairs were made with greater emphasis on their frames and especially remarkable was the show-wood frame of the back of the chair: the upholstered part was seen to protrude slightly from a deep surround of carved wood. These chairs were brightly gilded and when originally supplied must have had the splendid appearance of chased metal. The woodwork had by this time achieved a sculptural quality, a feature that had been derived from the Italians. In Venice, during the 1680s and 1690s, Andrea Brustolon made a magnificent suite of furniture for the Venier family which is now in the Palazzo Rezzonico. These pieces are totally sculptural in conception; items such as a vase stand or torchere are clearly independent carved objects but an armchair necessarily has to remain a thing with a purpose. The boxwood and ebony framework of Brustolon's model is not carved with the putti we might expect on Italian furniture of the period but in the form of gnarled tree trunks and branches. The arms are supported by nubians with ebony heads

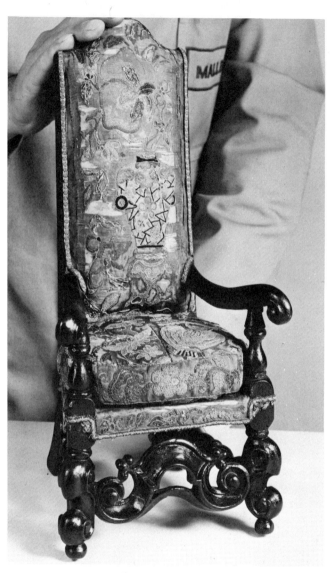

17th-century child's chair.

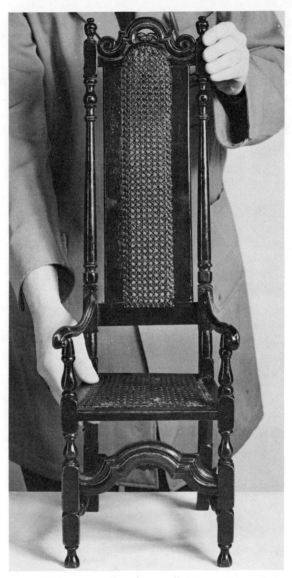

A very unusual late seventeenth-century small chair, possibly made for a doll.

and arms and ebony legs showing through their torn breeches of boxwood. Another chair, again sculptural in design and also outside the usual art of chair-making is the silver throne of King Frederick IV of Denmark. This fine piece, part of a suite made in Augsburg, is of wood covered with silver plating, a feature of a number of special commissions carried out in several countries. It has a high back crested with the Danish royal arms including both Sweden and Norway. The front legs are supported by crouched sphinxes. Much silver furniture was melted down in times of need. Several sets of silver furniture survive in England but I do not know of another silver chair of this period.

The Restoration of Charles II as King in England brought, or at least signalled, a turning point in many facets of artistic standards and craftsmanship. Oak had been the wood chiefly used for furniture-making and beech for upholstered chairs – beech is particularly prone to woodworm, hence the relatively few survivors – but now much greater use was made of the delightful 'walnutree'. Walnut had several advantages. Firstly, it was of a finer natural colour and figuration and could be polished, in either solid or veneer form, to an even warmer varied texture – a mellow brown. Secondly, it is a wood which grows in a variety of burr forms which can be thinly cut into veneers for decorating flat surfaces. This gnarled, curly, appearance was to be a specially sought-after quality and added a further dimension to the textured colour of the piece. It was not normally used on rounded parts such as chair legs which would be of solid timber but was used sparingly in veneer form on flat parts such as the back splats of chairs, drawer fronts, table tops and so on. It was largely from Holland, as in so many other respects, that England adopted the use of walnut, and in this case she perfected it.

Charles II chairs are identified by several notable features. In earlier and simpler examples, some of the frame, sometimes almost all of it, is composed of 'barley sugar' spiral turnings. The use of canework, as a basis for loose upholstered cushions, was a commonplace, the cane being of a coarse mesh and thickly cut. This cane was imported by the East India Company and was exceedingly popular; it gave a lightness of appearance to seat furniture and was tough and durable at least for several years. The new simplicity of construction led to the manufacture of sets of chairs, sometimes quite extensive. Two armchairs might be made with six, eight or more single chairs en suite. The popularity of the vogue was largely based on the plain fact that they were comfortable.

Other chairs were especially notable for their high backs and decorative woodwork. The caned seat and back were flanked by solid walnut panels richly carved and pierced with representations in fairly diminutive form of entwined amorini amongst foliate scrolling. Sometimes these infants supported a crown in the cresting of the top back rail and in the similarly shaped wide stretcher between the front legs. Other motifs included fruit and birds. Important chairs had carved animals resting on the arms. An example in the Victoria and Albert Museum, London has a crowned female bust in the cresting and stretcher as well as seated heraldic lions on the arm ends. The finials of the back posts are in the form of heads in theatrical or paper crowns. Another chair in the same museum displays slightly later tastes with, instead of barley sugar back posts, tapering rounded columns, and an arcaded front stretcher. Both chairs have scroll arms, resting on scroll supports, but the latter chair instead of the similar scroll front legs has more decorative legs with birds' heads at the knees and outward scrolling feet. A pascal lamb is shown in the cresting. All the carving is wonderfully rich, even where it is in bas-relief as on the column posts of the back. Fine chairs such as these reflect in large part the flamboyance of the restored King's reign.

Dutch chairs differed only slightly being a little heavier in form: the spiral turning was thicker and the arms and legs were bolder. They often had oval panels of canework in the backs and the carving was more complex and perhaps crisper in execution.

With the accession of William and Mary to the English throne further close connections were established with the Low Countries. Chair designs became distinctly more elegant and refined. In place of the flamboyant carving more emphasis was placed on the flowing scroll lines of arms, stretchers and crestings, while sobriety was also shown in the thin tapering back posts adopted in place of the barley sugar design. If anything there was a tendency to make the chair

An early 18th-century Dutch lacquer chair.

backs even taller. Lacquering, in imitation of the Chinese became very popular. Imported chests and screens had been much prized for some time but now European amateurs and professionals alike carried out imitations which captured the spirit of the decoration even if it did

A Queen Anne walnut wing chair. c. 1710.

not equal it in quality. In fact, European chinoiserie reached heights of great excellence in the reign of Queen Anne. A book entitled *A Treatise of Japanning and Varnishing* written by John Stalker and George Parker in 1688 led to great enthusiasm for the art and to examples such as the pair of chairs in Plate 6. In looking at these we also note that a new element of elegance was brought about by much finer canework – very thin strands woven in close mesh. The standard pattern of caning adopted during the eighteenth century and still used was somewhat less fine and less closely woven.

The late seventeenth century is also remembered for its rich textiles and upholstery. The materials used on chairs included damask, figured Genoa velvet, embroidered silk, fine needlework, brocatelle, brocade and elaborate trimmings and fringes. These materials often incorporated glistening gold and silver thread. Some good examples of such upholstery survive at houses such as Knole Park, Kent and Ham House, Surrey. At Ham there are very finely preserved chairs, some with pristine coverings, and also most interesting

'sleeping chayres, carv'd and gilt frames, covered with crimson and gould stuff with good fringes'.

Winged or Wing chairs were also made with high backs and large ear pieces for added comfort and draught protection. These had a minimal amount of woodwork showing at the legs and were heavily upholstered. Day beds or couches were also used and were of similar form to contemporary chairs. They had a raked back and this and the long flat part were usually caned, with cushions, or totally upholstered. Sofas and love seats were also made, being on the whole extended versions of the wing-chair form.

The greatest single influence on chair designs and the first man to have made an impression as such was Daniel Marot. A French Huguenot, Marot fled to Holland as a refugee and was there employed by Prince William of Orange as his architect and interior designer. Marot's drawings became enormously revered and helped to inspire many types of furniture. Chairs 'in the style of Daniel Marot' had smaller rounded backs with panels of closely composed intricate carving. The general shape gradually developed a new curvi-

DEVELOPMENT of the CABRIOLE LEG
c1695-1760

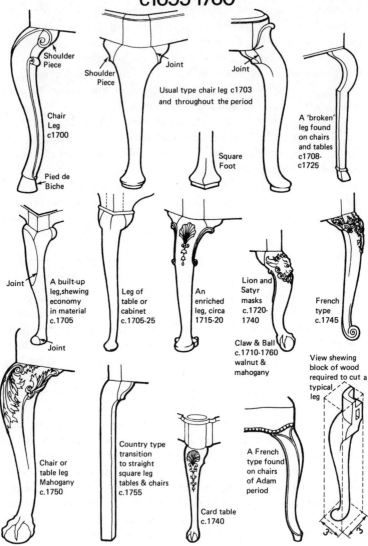

Shoulder Piece

Chair Leg c1700

Pied de Biche

Shoulder Piece

Joint

Usual type chair leg c1703 and throughout the period

Square Foot

Joint

A 'broken' leg found on chairs and tables c1708-c1725

Joint

A built-up leg, shewing economy in material c1705

Joint

Leg of table or cabinet c1705-25

An enriched leg, circa 1715-20

Lion and Satyr masks c1720-1740

French type c1745

Claw & Ball c1710-1760 walnut & mahogany

Chair or table leg Mahogany c1750

Country type transition to straight square leg tables & chairs c1755

Card table c.1740

A French type found on chairs of Adam period

View shewing block of wood required to cut a typical leg

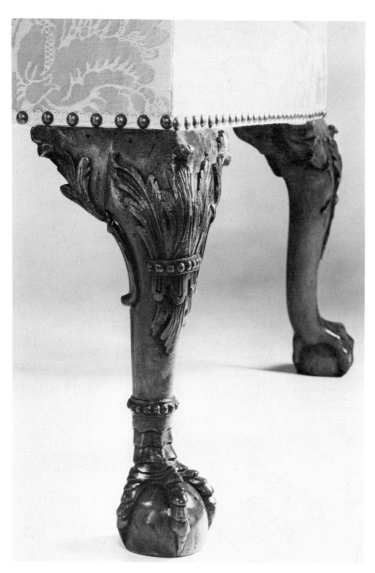

A finely carved cabriole chair leg.

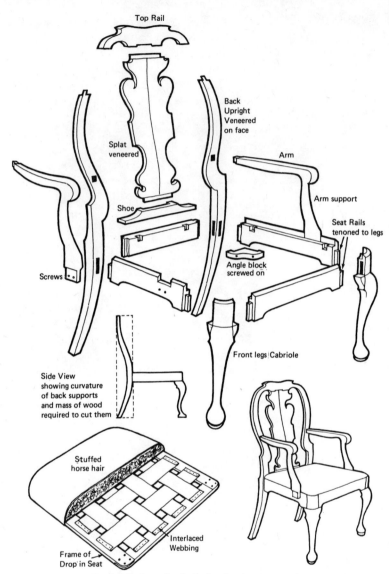

Top Rail

Back
Upright
Veneered
on face

Splat
veneered

Arm

Shoe

Arm support

Seat Rails
tenoned to legs

Screws

Angle block
screwed on

Front legs Cabriole

Side View
showing curvature
of back supports
and mass of wood
required to cut them

Stuffed
horse hair

Interlaced
Webbing

Frame of
Drop in Seat

Exploded view of a chair showing its components.

linear outline and notably, cabriole legs. This type of curved serpent leg, turning and tapering to a foot of various forms from a larger knee joint was given the name cabriole as late as the nineteenth century, the term having been adopted from late Georgian usage when it referred to a kind of armchair with a stuffed back. It is generally agreed that the leg itself derives, to some extent, from the shape of an animal's leg, and it often terminates in a hoof or claw. Animal legs and feet had, of course, been used on furniture in various parts of the world over several ages. Newly introduced in chair-making in Europe, it gave a new impetus to designs. It was above all a strong, elegant form with the commonsense advantages of practical stress engineering. At the same time the back of the chair developed a free dividing splat in the middle so that there would be two panels of canework or some-times just open spaces. The shape of the splat represented approxi-mately a vase and might be joined to the curvilinear uprights by a cross member. These splats were at first flat and later, possibly follow-ing early Chinese models, were shaped to support the back more comfortably. They were sometimes pierced and carved to a greater or lesser degree, and ultimately finely veneered with choice walnut, and might have just a modest touch of leaf carving somewhere on the outer edge. This type of chair was perfected in the reign of Queen Anne and many would say that if any singular type was to mark the epitome of beauty and craftsmanship in chair-making, it was this. By this time the legs were sufficiently strong not to need stretchers and they terminated in a variety of elegant pad feet. There was little carving, if any, on them, and the seat was usually covered with needle-work either upholstered over the frame or on a loose-shaped frame which dropped into the outer framework of the chair. As the first decade of the eighteenth century wore on and the second came in, chairs were again slightly more decorated with additional carved motifs such as a shell on the top back rail or on the front knees, and acanthus leaves might ornament the sides of the splat or appear on the pad feet. The foot itself changed eventually even more definitely to a revival of the ancient claw or claw and ball form. Such features can be seen on the two chairs in Plates 22/23, both fine specimens.

Chairs, however, were not only made in magnificent walnut. For

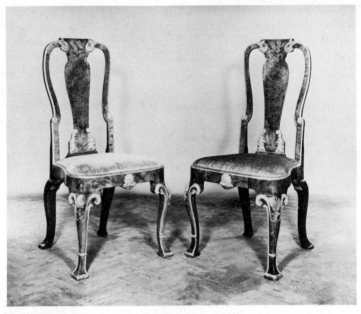

A pair of magnificent early 18th-century walnut side chairs with parcel gilding. c. 1715.

especially splendid rooms of a formal grandiose nature versions of giltwood were made or sometimes of walnut parcel-gilt (i.e. partially gilt). An especially magnificent gilt chair is illustrated in Plate 20. Originally from Benningborough Hall, this can be attributed to the royal maker James Moore, who was celebrated for his carved gesso furniture. The woodwork is coated with a number of layers of fine white plaster and this hard substance was carved and the background stamped with a ring pattern prior to overall water gilding. The ornament is especially rich and varied in this case. Perhaps even finer and with a better overall line is the gilt chair in Plate 21. To my mind this is the most beautiful of its kind. Two of the four William and Mary stools in Plates 7a, 8, 9a and 9b are parcel gilt and each reflect nuances of that period. Stools were still very popular during the age of walnut; rooms in great houses were often supplied

A pair of early 18th-century walnut side chairs upholstered with fine needlework. c. 1710.

with sets of stools. At Hampton Court Palace some rooms still have a number of stools and a solitary chair of state at one end.

As well as polished walnut and gilt gesso, many chairs were also decorated with lacquer in red, cream or black base colours with polychrome and gilt chinoiserie decoration. Giles Grendy is known to have made lacquer furniture for export to the continent; it seems that he had a particularly good trade with Spain. The red lacquer chairs in Plates 18/19 are attributed to his workshop.

Library and reading chairs were of differing forms. One kind with wide arms and fitted with an adjustable flap for supporting a book is sometimes referred to as a cockfighting chair. Another delightful sort had a small curved solid walnut or upholstered back and open arms, sometimes with a 'shepherd's crook' in the end. The three chairs in Plates 14, 15 and 16 illustrate these, the first two having interesting variations.

After the first two and half decades or so of the eighteenth century, walnut gradually became less fashionable and the newly imported mahogany became the vogue for new tastes. England, however, never produced a finer home product than the 'walnutree' seat furniture of the twenty-five years that began Europe's greatest artistic century.

4

French Elegance and Georgian Confidence

More wondrous still the table, stool and chair.

Much of the furniture of the first decades of the eighteenth century in Italy remained sculptural in essence. A fascinating carved and gilt armchair of about 1730, probably by Antonio Corradini of Venice can be seen at the Palazzo Rezzonico. It consists of a framework of figures, cherubs and cavorting horses, far removed from the more general art of chair-making which was developing in other parts of Europe.

In France a new sophisticated but relaxed taste emerged out of the pomp and stiffness of the court of Louis XIV, pursuing the comparative freedom of form of the rococo style. This was derived (in word and in mood) from the 'rocaille', rock formation, which was associated with Italianate grottoes. It reflected rocks, waterfalls, shells and often an element of chinoiserie in asymmetrical swirling forms, intermingled perhaps with animals ('singerie' – monkeys – particularly) and birds. These were the components of a fresh lightness of style and new humour in the form of furniture-making. Chairs especially were to reflect such trends; the larger cabinet pieces certainly were decorated with aspects of the new mood, but the smaller carved open form of chairs picked up especially quickly the new fashionable flavour. They show new flashes of imagination and exuberance, even frivolity, when compared with the fine products of the previous century. Classical antiquity was totally dismissed – at least for a while.

43

A pair of magnificent gilt rococo armchairs. English c. 1765.

Two Louis XV bergèrs.

A rare Louis XV walnut tub chair. c. 1760.

These new chairs were made to be in keeping with their room setting and to continue the feeling and decoration of the panelling on the walls, carved in flowing scrolls, probably painted and gilded. Usually of beechwood, they would be similarly decorated – the colours being much brighter than we know them nowadays, or indeed we should like today, and comfortably upholstered with soft stuffing and covered with fine silks. Comfort was a priority in the provision of chair-making and a wide variety of informal types of seat furniture was created.

'Fauteuils à la Reine' or 'meublents' had flat backs and were intended to be placed against the wall around a room; several variations derived from this type, such as certain 'chaises-longues'. These pieces were designed in keeping with the wall decoration, reflecting the ornamental motifs of the panelling. They were generally placed around the room for decorative purposes and not often sat on. On the other hand the 'courante' or 'en cabriolet' was by nature more relaxed and placed in the middle of the room for comfortable use, and such chairs were easily movable. The 'bergère' was even more welcoming, being larger with a cushioned seat and padded arms, sometimes with a folding back and adjustable book supports. Otherwise it might be curved more like the English tub chair. The 'duchesse-brisée' was a sort of day bed consisting of an armchair with a separate extension of the seat which could be drawn up to support the legs. This was a variant of the 'chaise longue'; it might alternatively have consisted of two armchairs and a stool between, or simply a single armchair with a much-extended seat, this latter being the form adopted in England in a modified state. A large bergère made for two to sit in was known as a 'tête-à-tête' or 'confident' or 'marquise'. A low chair which would be drawn up to the warm of the fire was a 'chauffeuse'. The 'fauteuil de bureau' had a curved front seat rail and an extra leg. A 'voyeuse' was for use at the games table. It had a padded back rail on which spectators could lean: a version without arms could be sat on back to front, like the English cock-fighting or library chair, while another type with a smaller seat could be used for kneeling on as is suggested by the name 'prie-dieu'. Office chairs were covered in leather fixed with studding and a variety of stools and benches were also used. Plainly utility chairs such as 'bidets' were also sometimes made with the utmost artistry and attention to detail.

On the whole other countries on the mainland of the continent did not contribute great developments in furniture design at this time but were largely influenced by French design and craftsmanship. Ger-

46

A Louis XV beechwood bergère.

many for example produced its own modified versions of the rococo style but these were chiefly inspired by French models. Similarly Holland was no longer at the forefront of innovation though its masterpieces had led European tastes in the previous half-century.

In England, however, a combination of factors led to a splendid outburst of creative progress in furniture design and in craftsmanship. By no means least amongst the various forms of furniture, chairs changed and developed rapidly and the several stages of the eighteenth century can be said to have produced a number of masterpieces representative of each. It was a great period for the decorative arts in England. The Georgian period was one, the only one I believe, when deisgners and craftsmen seemed to be driven by an intuitive good sense of proportion and rhythm. It seems that bad taste hardly existed. Architecture, furniture, music and literature all reflect a graceful quality that governed and represent the period. Further, I would venture to suggest that of all these, furniture-making and particularly chair-making showed especial variety.

The stimulus was in part derived from that splendid Dutch–English blend of the late seventeenth century and the use of walnut, lacquer and gesso but later it was effected by the use of a new material, mahogany. Mahogany had been known in England but was not used for furniture. However, in 1721 an Act of Parliament abolished the import duty on timber brought in from British colonies and this led to imports of mahogany from North America and the West Indies. Jamaica was encouraged to export not only its own wood but also quantities from San Domingo, Cuba and Puerto Rico. This new material is featured in the royal furniture accounts as soon as three years after the abolition of the levy, that is in 1724, but of course on the whole it took longer for the wood to be generally adopted.

In the meantime we may examine aspects of achievement in the years prior to the actual age of mahogany. The much favoured form of walnut side chairs with curvilinear backs changed slowly. The backs became lower and the seats wider to accommodate the elaborate stiffened costumes worn at the time by both men, with pleated coats, and women with hoop dresses. At the same time the use of ornament increased so that the decoration rather than the form itself was prominent. Gilded furniture particularly, displayed in England the influence of Italianate baroque elements. The epitome of this mood was reached by William Kent, an architect, whose magnificent interiors incorporated systematically, complete furnishing designs including

48

particularly mirrors with console tables to go beneath them or else-where. He also provided seat furniture, which was characterised, like the other items, by sea motifs such as dolphins, shells and a scale-pattern background. But overall his conception was architectural and his furniture, and that of his followers' furniture, was made to fit in with a classical type of interior. It was decorated with architectural mouldings, rosettes and scrolling, in particular Vitruvian wave-like scrolling. One of his masterpieces was his work on the interior of Houghton Hall, Norfolk and the furniture he supplied for that house. Several very fine sets of chairs dating from about 1730 are in Houghton Hall. Two are of carved and gilt wood and gesso, the bolder motifs being carved on the woodwork and the finer details being carved in the gesso coating, is the plaster preparation for the gilding. Each chair is also upholstered in crimson and rose coloured cut Italian velvet. One chair, with curved sides to the back, leans back to the tastes of earlier reigns while the other with more baroque-rococo features shows modern trends. Both have scroll arms but the former chair has the shaped back of Queen Anne origin and 'broken' cabriole legs. This chair is profusely carved with decoration: there are Indian head masks on the knees, a cluster of formal feathers at the top of the back, and swags of husks and the fish-scale pattern in low relief on other parts. The second chair is more typical but is an especially fine example of Kent's work. The straight back splaying out at the top is a feature newly introduced to England and the upright posts of this are decorated with overlapping rings. The arm-ends and the inwardly scrolling toes on the front legs are decorated with acanthus leaves. The scrolling around the seat rail, the masks on the knees and especially the shell motif in the front are hallmarks of Kent decoration.

Such elaborate sculptural work was not carried out in the newly introduced mahogany, which had its own virtues. It was hard and certainly lent itself well to crisp carving but it was close grained and of a good natural colour which would polish up well with attractive flat surfaces. In addition it was strong and woodworm free which has meant that it has survived relatively well compared to painted, gilt and walnut furniture. The grain was fairly plain and similar in texture and colour to Virginia Walnut. Much walnut furniture continued to be made till the middle of the century but the mahogany has survived better. Where the plain nature of the grain invited carving the motifs that were particularly popular included lions' heads on arm-ends and knees, lions' paw feet (not 'poor feet', as once typed in an antiques shop) or claw and ball feet, and animal legs of a stylised type.

A pair of grisaille hall chairs bearing the arms of the Duke of Leeds.

Eagle motifs are also seen in heads, legs and feet; and human and satyr masks, acanthus leaves, various mouldings and a cartouche pattern or catouchon, on knees. A fine Kentian set of mahogany seat furniture from Wroxton Abbey, Oxfordshire, of which a sofa is in the Victoria and Albert Museum, London, is carved with characteristic crispness. This settee is in triple-chair formation, a feature fairly common in England from this time onwards and the carved ornament is highlighted with parcel gilding.

Lacquer furniture continued to be made and England exported it to the continent as before, competing in favour with painted chairs, following French shapes, such as the Italian blue and gilt armchair

Two most unusual hoop backed japanned chairs. c. 1770.

in Plate 28. A very fine English gilt armchair, Plate 27, closely follows French rococo inspiration with shallow but florid carving.

Painted or mahogany hall chairs were made in sets and spaced around the walls of the entrance hall. They had no upholstery and were often of a stark strange neo-classical form, usually in keeping with the decoration of the room. Frequently they displayed on the backs in carving or with painted decoration either the crest or arms of the owner of the house. A quotation from *Brideshead Revisited* must be allowed here as it sums up such furniture so well:

'There was a little heraldic chair by the chimney-piece, one of a set which stood against the walls, a little, inhospitable, flat seated thing, a mere excuse for the elaborate armorial painting on its back, on which, perhaps, no one, not even a weary footman, had ever sat since it was made.'

With the 1740s new trends developed, noticeably chairs with pierced backs, still sometimes with a rounded top rail, but often with straight uprights on the sides of the back, widening slightly towards the top rail. Straight legs were re-introduced again in some cases and these called for the use again of stretchers. Generally we notice a sense of simplification, even if rococo in ornament, in reaction to the massive baroque S and C scrolling.

Though only one of a number of leading masters of furniture design, but something of a giant, was Thomas Chippendale 1718–79. In 1754 he produced a pattern book entitled *The Gentleman and Cabinet Maker's Director* which was immediately a great success and passed

Chippendale period mahogany side chairs in the Chinese taste.

A painted simulated bamboo armchair. c. 1770.

through several editions. It was widely distributed, having originally been subscribed to by the gentry. In this work the author showed in a wide range of drawings a variety of designs for a complete range of household furniture. It presented for public consumption and especially for craftsmen a composite view of the rococo style as seen through English eyes. It also showed designs 'in the Chinese manner'. The combination of rococo and chinoiserie elements produced one of the most satisfactory cross-blends and Chippendale is justly famed for his Chinese Chippendale chairs, even if they are not technically based on his designs. Pagoda back rails, lattice work chinoiserie backs, turned 'bamboo' legs in formal clusters (more like gothic columns) blind and open fret carving on square legs, bells, phoenix birds and icicles are all ingredients of these delightful concoctions. The armchair in Plate 32 and the side chair in Plate 34 show aspects of these features.

The *Director* also suggested fanciful 'ribband-back' or ribbon-back chairs but I believe relatively few of these were executed. They were widely faked in the nineteenth century but now seem sadly the least attractive of Chippendale's styles. His Gothic designs somehow lack the lightness of the type Horace Walpole preferred at Strawberry Hill around 1750 but again his drawings must only be seen as representative of one maker's view. Others produced copious suggestions. Robert Mainwaring, for example, issued two books entirely devoted to designs for chairs. In all the books attention is rightly given to varieties of cabriole leg with scrolling toes turning both ways, outwards and inwards, 'French' designs, varieties of top rails in the form of a cupid's bow, and serpentine front seat rails – following Hogarth's ideal 'serpentine line, or line of grace'. But many other less 'woody' chairs were also made that are not so strongly featured in the drawing books, such as large Gainsborough armchairs, comfortable for reading in; plainer wing chairs, descendants of the Queen Anne type; and countless other kinds with small variations. Examples of the Gainsborough type are shown in Plates 30, 31 and 35. The continental rococo taste is seen in a very fine English giltwood armchair of about 1760 (see Plate 29), with excited sculptural broken scrolls flowing in and out of each other. The Louis XV form was often adopted without

An unusual oak Chippendale gothic armchair. c. 1765.

any adaptation; chairs like the pair from Harewood House, Yorkshire, where Chippendale is known to have worked, could easily be mistaken as French (see Plates 38/39). They are similar in form to the other set of Louis XV chairs shown in Plates 48/49. A further pair

A fine Chippendale mahogany side chair. c. 1760.

of English mahogany armchairs of the same type, with gadrooning carved decoration, is illustrated in Plate 41.

Beyond Europe, English influences led to interesting varieties and strangely there was not much of a time-lag in fashions. For example in

Detail of the carved back.

America, Chippendale-style chairs seem to have been produced from about 1760. Fine Philadelphia specimens are closely related to designs in Chippendale's *Director*. Of solid mahogany, these chairs had a good line, drop in upholstered seats and were finely carved very much in the English manner but with slight nuances that are hardly distinguishable but give them an overall individuality. Of the chair illustrated it might be observed that it has a fairly thick, flat seat rail with an emphasised shell motif in the centre (an inheritance of earlier

One of a pair of Chippendale wing chairs.

curvilinear-back chairs of the walnut type), a carved tassel in the centre of the pierced slat and a gadrooned 'shoe' moulding at the base of the splat. Chairs of similar quality were also made in Massachusetts, especially Boston, and to some extent in New York and Newport. Prior to the 'Chippendale'-style chair there was a general tradition of furniture of the 'Queen Anne' type, which in America persisted until around 1750. Chairs with hooped backs containing flat-shaped splats and with only a carved shell motif on the top rail and knees were made chiefly of mahogany and had drop-in seats. They were of heavier construction than their English or Dutch counterparts.

More exotic 'English' chairs were made even further afield. In India, European fashions were mimicked from imported examples or from prints and drawings, sometimes for use locally and sometimes for export. Two splendid chairs in ivory may be cited. Plate 36 shows one of a pair of round-back solid ivory chairs with engraved and gilded decoration. Another chair of sandalwood and ivory, one of a colossal set is in the Royal Collection at Buckingham Palace. Many English motifs are reflected in these, but emblems such as the dragon heads in the back with red lacquer mouths are totally oriental in inspiration. This set of furniture was made in Madras around 1770 for the then Governor of Fort St George and was bought by George III in 1781. It was later placed in Brighton Pavilion by George IV.

5

The Climax of Quality and Beyond

Thus first necessity invented stools,
Convenience next suggested elbow-chairs,
And luxury the accomplish'd sofa last.

The zenith of fine chair-making was reached in the second half of the eighteenth century with several varying forms which combined beautiful designs with an excellence of craftsmanship. Patterns based on rococo inspiration but further freed by a French lightness and natural sophistication of line, and others with brilliant English creative features, produced delightful masterpieces. A splendid variety of forms incorporating different shapes in backs, arms and legs, ranging in decorative technique from crisply carved decoration and richly polished wood to gilding and painting and lacquering in the Chinese manner.

Craftsmanship continued to become more and more impressive, with an increased use of inlay, not so much in the form of marquetry, at least not floral marquetry, (as perfected in Holland in the seventeenth century) but in simpler line decoration combined with complex uses of contrasting cross-bandings. Design also developed into two more distinct categories, firstly elaborately decorated forms of neo-classical inspiration, and secondly a lighter delicate style suited to more general use.

The greatest importance in the gradual transition of tastes through the climax of chair-making to the beginning of the end of its magnificence was the new craze which fascinated professionals and amateurs, artists and patrons alike. This was neo-classicism.

In 1738 the ruins of Herculaneum were discovered and in 1749 Pompeii. All Europe became involved in some way in discovering and spreading news of the culture of these ancient and other classical sites. Madame de Pompadour's brother, later to become Superintendent of Fine Arts, went on a tour of Italy to study the subject and Madame du Barry became enthusiastic about the new cult. The engravings of Piranesi with exaggerated grandeur displayed reconstructions of the buildings that were now discovered in ruins. He and art students from all over Europe combed over details and fragments of architecture, the motifs used in decoration, pieces of utensils, vases and furniture that were newly unearthed and reconsidered many remains already known. Robert Adam, a Scotsman by birth, was amongst these enthusiasts, as were the painters David and Hubert Robert of France. The influence of this new interest soon showed itself in furniture-making and became of paramount importance over the next sixty or seventy years. Firstly the ideas were used as the basis of highly decorative ornament and later, in the nineteenth century in a purer academic format more closely related to the actual archaeological evidence and remains.

The general spirit affected most European countries. France and England were at the centre of creative production and as a result showed especially a development of new styles. It is difficult to say which country first showed leanings of preference to neo-classic design: in France the rococo taste carried on quite fashionably alongside the new craze until the end of the ancien régime, while in England a gradual and happy merging took place over a transitional period rather than a co-existence.

Robert Adam (1728–92) was not the first to use neo-classical motives in England but he became the greatest exponent of the style. Earlier introduction had been made by James 'Athenian' Stuart and by Sir William Chambers. The latter designed the President's chair for the Royal Society of Arts in 1759 with several bold classical elements, most noticeably round tapering front legs with spiral fluting, and also with bas-relief carving in the form of classical Vitruvian scrolls and the overlapping ring or money pattern. Adam on return from his tour and encouraged by his study of ancient and also Renaissance art in Italy, became the leading spirit amongst a number of architects, designers and designer craftsmen who actually carried out and perfected ideas he germinated. It should be mentioned and stressed that though Chippendale is justly famous through his *Director* for rococo furniture, he was also a master of the later neo-classical form and many would say that his masterpieces were in this field. It is known that his workshops produced a greater quantity in this vogue than in the earlier rococo manner and also that he was responsible for the actual production of furniture to Robert Adam's designs. Amongst Chippendale's own patrons was the Earl of Harewood and the furniture that Chippendale made for his house in Yorkshire is amongst the most important ever made, being superbly inlaid with delicately shaded woods in beautifully ordered neo-classical patterns.

Robert Adam was essentially an architect though he also provided detailed drawings for every aspect of the interior decoration of a room. His earlier furniture designs show transitional cross references. A giltwood armchair in the Victoria and Albert Museum, London, for example, is of rococo outline but is decorated with the anthemion (honeysuckle) motif and sphinxes. When he applied himself to more thorough interiors his basic furniture, that around the walls for instance, was largely architectural and was conceived to be in keeping with all the structural fixtures such as the door cases. By the time his style was fully evolved, his houses (frequently most successful adaptations of earlier buildings) were carefully united through every detail from gate lodges to fire grates. Osterley Park, Middlesex, has rooms that are among his finest achievements. They contain magnificent furniture. Much of which was copiously designed by Adam while some pieces were made by John Linnell. There are many fine chairs in the house, and they display all the finest characteristics of the period. A fascinating library armchair, one of a set (as are all these Osterley chairs), has the lyre back which was an English innovation. The framework of the chair is of mahogany but is elaborately veneered with crossbanding and inlays of other woods that depict several specifically neo-classical ornaments – Vitruvian scrolls, swags of husks, crossed palm leaves, stylised flutings and flattened scrolls on the arm supports. The chair is further enriched with a gilt metal

A fine Louis XVI armchair.

portrait medallion and swags around the front legs. Four other chairs show similar features carried out in different ways. A dining chair has a transitional 'Chippendale' look but the carved decoration is of the mood of the house. A fine giltwood armchair has an oval back, derived from French Louis XV models, and is supported at the base by a pair of winged sphinxes. The quality and nature of the other parts is very French and is beautifully proportioned and exe-cuted. Of quite a different character again is a square-backed painted beechwood armchair in the Etruscan taste. This form of decoration, carried out throughout an entire room at Osterley, was derived from the decoration on Greek vases. Other than this it has no true precedent but the idea developed independently in the delight for 'antique' settings. The patterns used combine a curious mixture of cultural elements with a predominant terra cotta colour, in this case on a white background. A giltwood version of a square-back armchair, made for Northumberland House (where Adam was also employed) is shown in Plate 51b. Hallmarks of the school of furniture makers that was led by Adam are easily discernible and are closely associated with Louis XVI counterparts. They include especially anthemion (honeysuckle), swags of husks, fluting in profusion, draperies, paterae (rosettes) and wheat ears. Though chinoiserie lacquer was no longer favoured for chairs, they were frequently painted in plainer decora-tive colours such as green and white, blue and white, or in single colours. (See PLATE 57)

The other chief exponent of chair design in the second half of the eighteenth century in England was George Hepplewhite whose *Cabinet Maker and Upholsterer's Guide* was published posthumously in 1788. This work popularised to some extent, as Sheraton was later to continue, an overall gracefulness. It is for this quality that Hepple-white is especially remembered. His name brings to mind light designs with shield-shaped, heart-shaped and square backs; with square tapering legs, upholstered or carved seats (with squab cushions), no stretchers; and the backs filled with open wheatsheaf splats and plain upright rail formations. It is probable that Hepplewhite was the first to advocate the use of Prince of Wales feathers as a decorative motif. This became widely popular and was usually incorporated in a

Portrait of
King Richard
II sitting on a
mediaeval
Gothic style
throne.

2   The gilt throne of Tutankhamun
made 3,300 years ago.

3a Tutankhamun's wood and gilt stool.

3b Upholstered sofa at Knole House, Sevenoaks, Kent. Late 17th-century.

4   Charles II oak armchair with lions carved on the arms.

5   Elaborate triangular 'thrown' or turned bobbin chair. Early 17th-century.

6   A pair of high-backed William and Mary armchairs, c. 1690.

7a A pair of finely carved late 17th-century parcel gilt walnut stools.

7b An early 18th-century walnut stool with needlework seat.

8   A William and Mary walnut stool.

9a   A William and Mary walnut stool with crossed stretchers.

9b   A Queen Anne or George I walnut parcel gilt stool.

10a   A Dutch walnut and marquetry sofa and armchair. Early 18th-century.

11a   **Opposite:** A pair of Queen Anne side chairs with stretchers.

11b   **Opposite:** A pair of Queen Anne side chairs with cabriole legs.

10b   A pair of William and Mary red lacquer side chairs.

12   An early 18th-century cream lacquer side chair.

13   A Dutch black lacquer side chair.

14   A Queen Anne walnut armchair.

15   A Shepherd's crook armchair. Early 18th-century.

16   An early 18th-century walnut library or cock-fighting chair.

17 An oval Queen Anne walnut stool with cabriole legs.

18 & 19   Two of a set of chairs attributed to Giles Grendy, c. 1715.

20 An important early 18th-century carved gilt gesso chair.

21 A magnificent gilt gesso side chair of about 1720.

22   A George I walnut side chair, c. 1720.

23 George I chair in walnut with needlework seat, c. 1720.

24a   A Queen Anne gilt and carved gesso sofa.

24b   A pair of carved giltwood armchairs in the French taste. English
         c. 1770.

25 An early 18th-century carved gilt gesso wing chair.

26   An early 18th-century walnut wing chair.

27   An important rococo giltwood armchair, c. 1740.

28   A mid 18th-century Italian painted armchair.

29   A fine Chippendale rococo armchair, c. 1750.

30 A carved giltwood Gainsborough armchair mid 18th-century.

31　A Chippendale Gainsborough armchair of mahogany.

32 A Chippendale mahogany armchair in the Chinese taste.

33 A Chippendale mahogany side chair, c. 1765.

34   A Chinese Chippendale side chair upholstered with fine needlework.

35   A mid 18th-century mahogany Gainsborough armchair with fish scale
carving.

36   An 18th-century Indian ivory chair with five legs.

37a   A pair of giltwood Italian armchairs made in Lucca c. 1780.

37b   A pair of Italian Piedmontese side chairs c. 1770.

38/39   A pair of English armchairs in the French taste.

40　An Italian neo-classical painted armchair.

41   A fine mahogany armchair with gadrooning decoration, c. 1770.

42/43   A pair of Adam style giltwood armchairs and a foot stool en suite,
c. 1780.

44 A fine Adam period painted armchair.

45 **Opposite:** A Sheraton shield-back armchair with Prince of
Wales feathers in the back. c. 1775.

46/47   Part of a set of simulated bamboo seat furniture. 18th-century.

48/49   A set of four Louis XV fauteuils or armchairs, c. 1760.

50a   A pair of small Louis XVI side chairs with arched backs.

50b   Two late 18th-century giltwood chairs, part of a set.

51a Two of a set of white and gilt chairs in the manner of James Wyatt.

51b Two of a set of Adam giltwood chairs in the Louis XVI manner from
      Northumberland House. c. 1780.

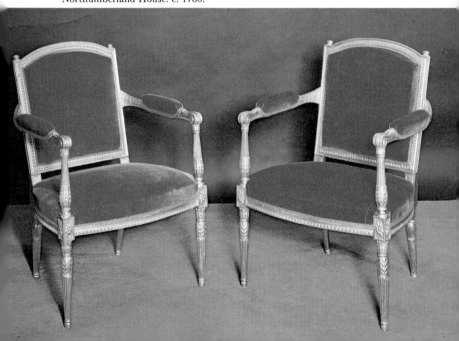

52 An Indian solid ivory armchair, c. 1790.

53 A fine mahogany tub chair, c. 1780.

54a   A pair of Regency armchairs and a dolphin centre table. English, *c.* 1810.

54b   A pair of Russian side chairs, with brasswork decoration, c. 1780.

55a   A fine pair of Adam giltwood armchairs, c. 1770.

55b   A pair of English armchairs in the form of Louis XV bergeres, c. 1780.

56   A late 18th-century armchair upholstered with tapestry.

57   A blue and white painted side chair, c. 1790.

58a   A pair of Regency chairs probably designed by Georgé Smith, c. 1810.

58b   A pair of William IV maroon lacquer chairs.

59   A Sheraton painted armchair, c. 1790.

60 A Regency armchair with unusual Greek-Etruscan motifs, c. 1815.

61 An early 19th-century giltwood X-frame armchair with birds' heads carving.

62   An inlaid chair with Art Nouveau influence designed by Bugatti.

63a   A pair of comfortable deep buttoned chairs, c. 1840.

63b   A red lacquer Art Nouveau
          side chair, c. 1890.

63c   A high-backed chair
          designed by C. R.
          Mackintosh, c. 1900.

64   An Art Nouveau child's chair.

small form at the top of the back of the chair. One of a finely executed and rare pair of shield-back mahogany chairs with Prince of Wales feathers, bound together by a coronet, is illustrated in Plate 45. The crisp, bold carving of the feathers is delightful; they are unusually large, filling the entire shield-back of the chair.

Hepplewhite seat furniture is often associated with graceful cabriole

A very fine pair of Hepplewhite mahogany armchairs. c. 1775.

legs of a light kind and flowing curved backs as seen on sofas and bergères or tub chairs.

Thomas Sheraton (1757–1806), from a journeyman, rose through the ranks to become another famous exponent of taste. His *Drawing Book* was issued in parts and was much subscribed to and widely influential. It brought fashionable ideas with delicate middle-class association into more popular circulation. The designs suggested less showy and less expensive forms that suited the country at a time when money was short, following a long and costly war with France. Straight lines, square backs, slender tapering round legs turning outwards slightly near the toes and an overall vertical emphasis, rather than the previous horizontal, was now the vogue. The arms often had a graceful sweep up into the back rails and another sweep below into thin columns going into the seat or extended through the seat down the legs. Although Sheraton advocated the use of satinwood for much

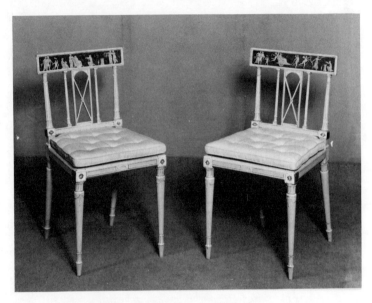

A pair of Sheraton painted occasional side chairs. c. 1800.

cabinet-making, it appears that it was not much used for chairs. When it was, it was often superimposed with floral paintwork. Many chairs were totally painted in bright, cheerful and contrasting colours and many were decorated in black with gold decoration. This type of japanning sought to follow a more archaeological approach to neo-classicism, an approach which unconsciously disapproved of the eclectic mixture of the Adam style. At this point the Regency period had arrived and in style it was more or less equivalent to the Directoire and Empire styles in France. Before examining it, however, we must refer to the Louis XVI developments that were running alongside the English fashions.

Following the initial interest shown by the nobility and art students alike the neo-classical craze caught on with wide effect in France, though as I have said, it co-existed with a continued appreciation of rococo forms. In some ways the new mood showed less in chair-making than it did in cabinets, for the two fields have important differences and were always separated. While commodes were ven-eered, decorated with complex marquetry and carried elaborate ormolu mounts, chairs were of solid wood with no mounts and dec-orated solely with carving and painting or gilding. It was their basic shape that was important and this often changed less radically. The leading painters already mentioned, David and Hubert Robert, both conceived designs for chairs which were realised by Georges Jacob. He was not only a cabinet-maker but also an important chair-maker and joiner – Menuisier.

Louis XVI chairs were sometimes of polished wood, occasionally parcel gilded, but more often either painted or gilt or a combination of paint and gilt. The most popular form had a square back, arms with upholstered pads and tapering legs either round or square with fluting in a straight up and down or spiralling manner. Balloon-back chairs, originally celebrating the first Paris flights of the Montgolfiers' balloon, were popular with a pierced central splat not unlike the wheatsheaf pierced backs on English chairs. These balloon chairs would not have arms. An attractive pair closely derived from the balloon-shaped back are illustrated in Plate 50a. The French usually upholstered their chairs at this time with silks, damask or velvet but seldom with tapestry. Italian chairs were a little different and were especially interesting in the Piedmont region. Side chairs often had the squared formality and neo-classical decoration that might be expected. The grisaille armchair in Plate 40 is more exotic with interesting spiralled legs. Another pair of chairs on the same page, entirely gilt were made in Lucca and bear the maker's label. These are a foretaste of the more elaborately carved Regency type; the curled-up leaf

A Louis XVI beechwood chair.

motif within the arms was something of a feature of chairs from this area. (See PLATE 37a)

From the Louis XVI style and the English corresponding period there followed in France the Directoire and Empire styles and in England the Regency style. Both were born out of a new approach to neo-classicism. The contrived use of elements of decoration applied to very European models in a fairly arbitrary mixture was frowned upon and in its place designers began to attempt a more scholarly approach in following archaeological evidence. They tried to copy ancient models as closely as possible and created their versions – with decorative motives that they felt were appropriate.

Three Regency black and gold chairs. c. 1810.

In France Napoleon's desire, to assert and establish his prestige through the arts, expressed itself in very much the same enthusiastic way as did Louis XIV, whom the emperor so hoped to emulate. His search for majesty and grandeur knew no bounds and was reflected in the elaborately made and symbolic throne-like chairs based on ancient models. Jacob's Etruscan-style chairs of mahogany with a curved flat back panel, decorated with Graeco-Roman painting as on a vase perhaps, were of the noble nature that suited the near deification of Napoleon. The klismos too, based on a Greek model, and with a similar but even more curved (semi-circular) back panel was an academic revival. The 'curule' was another popular form; it had X-frame legs crossing from one side to the other. The 'gondola' was a

An 18th-century mahogany child's chair. c. 1770.

kind of tub chair and a delightful pair of these at Malmaison show another fashionable emblem, the swan, in the arms, while the same is repeated in the fine patterned silk covering of the upholstery. These chairs are beautifully painted and gilded but less important examples were of fine woods, polished and with well-chased ormolu

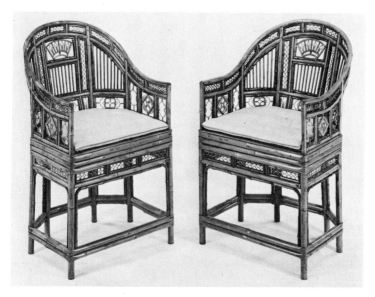

A pair of Chinese rattan tub chairs. c. 1810.

mounts. There was little or no marquetry and the general effect was sober and academic.

In England the neo-classical origins were similarly culled in a search for purer style and again the chief influences were the discoveries of old forms in Egypt, Greece and Rome. Napoleon's campaign in Egypt and Nelson's victory on the Nile fed back ideas and brought about commemorative elements. As in France animal forms were incorporated profusely: chimeras, winged lions, sphinxes, dragons and all sorts of wild beasts from snakes to crocodiles were depicted

A mahogany exercising chair.

in carving and in mounts. The monopoid lion was a popular English emblem and was used notably by George Smith as on a pair of tub chairs, illustrated in Plate 58a. George Smith's *Collection of Drawings* ... (1808) gathered together for general use many of the prevalent ideas, and included the Greek klismos. Severity was also shown in Thomas Hope's *Household Furniture and Interior Decoration* of 1807 which illustrates his own rich collection of specially ordered furniture.

Despite the somewhat austere taste that these aims attracted there were as well the more frivolous creations of the Chinese and Gothic manner. Furniture in the form of bamboo, that is of wood, carved and painted to simulate bamboo had been popular since about 1770 but now the Prince Regent (later George IV) and his architect Henry Holland conceived at the Royal Pavilion at Brighton a splendid cavort of humour and exotic fantasy to beat the wildest of imaginations. The Prince imported Chinese rattan furniture and thereby set a precedent for a craze that is still popular and had made a colossal range of furniture in extraordinary bizarre forms. This was the height of Regency creation even if it was largely based on frivolous eccentricity. The lesser more permanent achievements showed signs of a weakening in invention. Trafalgar chairs, for example, were made of a type that could easily be duplicated and therefore gradually became debased. The original version, commemorating the battle of that name and decorated with a rope motif on the back top rail, and perhaps the uprights as well, was an elegant but simple carved chair with sabre legs, curving inwards and out at the feet in concave form. However, from this it was coarsened and took on less elegant members and poorly designed and worked brass inlay. Other Regency and Empire shapes were also outplayed and became ridiculously exaggerated, impractical for proper use and lacking in the imaginative spark that only survived in this style for a limited period. It had been an offshoot of the great Georgian and Louis XV and XVI era, but in itself it could not give birth to or lead to a major new development.

6

Quantity and Confusion

Stretch'd on the rack of a too easy chair.

The year 1830 is often taken as an arbitrary date to divide 'classic' antiques from merely 'late' furniture. Even if this is increasingly unfair as time goes by and of less importance that date does approximately represent the time when standards showed something of a change in approach. It marks the period when style was fairly decisively de-bunked in favour of a popular search for comfort: the beginning of a move towards the easy chair, with its shape in a secondary place, often relegated to general confusion and ugliness. On the whole design has developed in a struggling desperate way through the nineteenth and twentieth centuries, constantly looking back through revivals and nostalgia to idealised periods, but not sure or confident of its destiny and not producing a convincing and happy progressive style.

As Regency and Empire forms grew debased and lost the vitality that they originally had they took on ridiculous exaggerated charac-teristics that made chairs neither practical nor handsome. Many now look something of a joke; others gradually became coarse and dull. As the standards of design fell, craftsmanship on the contrary, improved with the aid of better tools and methods and eventually with the development of machines that assisted in perfecting certain hand crafts such as cutting wood, veneers, etc. Such implements also helped to face the challenge of increased demands especially in supplying ever growing quantities of furniture for the larger number of people who now wanted fashionable modern things. At the same time

A 19th-century satinwood armchair in the gothic taste.

materials were increasingly easy to procure; fine woods were brought to European countries from their colonies and other countries with more and more efficiency. The Industrial Revolution in England and corresponding developments of mechanisation and commerce in Europe raised the standard of living for very many people. They did not, strangely, choose to emulate and extend the Georgian era with its obviously fine qualities but looked upon those as having a stagnating 'uniformity'. Instead they sought a more romantic approach to older established virtues and qualities. Ludon's *Encyclopaedia* (1833) indicated that the main styles in vogue at the time were Grecian, Gothic, Elizabethan and Louis XIV. The Grecian was an extension of Regency 'neo-classicism'; the Gothic likewise had Regency roots but had taken on religious and Romantic overtones; the Elizabethan was only partly Tudor, it was also largely late Stuart revival and the Louis XIV represented another craving for an element of the grandiose. To these might also shortly have been added nineteenth-century versions of Renaissance and Louis XV styles. The former was a dull revival and at its weakest when popular early in the present century. The latter was a return to rococo ideas, and the only eighteenth-century form to have been taken up again. It led to huge popularity in mahogany furniture, cabinets and chairs alike in high Victorian England (1860–1900). But in the revival of all these styles there can be seen in retrospect a sad confusion of overall style, which was inevitably linked with the obvious problems and pitfalls caused by the greater production that was required of chair-makers and others. There were, of course, some fine chairs made in all parts after the earlier part of the nineteenth century but generally the standard was based on new credentials that have today a sense of quaintness, but not quality. In some countries including France, the old eighteenth-century models continued to be made in an atmosphere of conservatism, in much the same way that in Ireland Georgian architecture remained the fashion for builders in Dublin and other outlying places. Such chairs as these are, of course, not reproductions in the disparaging sense of the word, but they would not rank with examples of the true period.

In England, the Grecian-style chair, based, as already stated, on

A French carved wood chair, 1867, perhaps a model for a cast iron version.

Regency foundations, was extremely popular. It had a curved flat horizontal back with perhaps a parallel stretcher below, and the legs were turned and tapered. These chairs lent themselves in design to mass production and many large sets were made for dining-rooms or parlours, with only minor differences in outline and ornament. They

An early 19th-century gothic white and gold chaise longue.

were efficient but dull. Gothic chairs are more interesting. They were derived from the 'gothick' of Strawberry Hill and the Regency period, but had none of the lightness and frivolity of either. Instead they showed a reference back, with a note of pseudo-archaeological scholarship, to mediaeval Gothic styles and had in many cases a distinctly religious air. They were decorated with a combination of tracery, buttresses, pinnacles, crockets and other motifs. A. W. N. Pugin, who designed the new Houses of Parliament with Sir Charles

Barry was the best designer in this style and was the originator of much fine furniture with a Gothic flavour for these buildings. Perhaps because so much furniture was required to be made for the Houses of Parliament, the designs are for the most part unencumbered with much unnecessary detail and for this reason have a modest combination of style and functional qualities. At this point I might also refer the reader again to the throne in the House of Lords, which in contrast is highly decorated (in both senses of the word), and is an interesting nineteenth-century example of mediaevalism. It is to be compared with great mediaeval thrones such as the Coronation Chair.

The Elizabethan-style chairs, that were in fact just as much Jacobean, had reminiscent tall backs and barley sugar, spiral-turned legs and uprights on the backs. In the place of carving, the backs and seats, and sometimes the arms too, were often padded deeply with upholstery.

Upholstery was of great importance in the manufacture of Victorian chairs, sofas and other seating. Comfort was the paramount requisite and consequently designs were shaped by the necessary emphasis on upholstery. This ultimately led to totally 'soft furnishing'. From the early nineteenth century plushly padded seats and luxurious covering fabrics were a feature of the best chairs and to some extent, and increasingly, the upholstery was allowed to become an important part of the piece from a stylistic as well as practical point of view. The tightly stretched upholstery of the seats and backs of eighteenth-century models and the squat cushions on caned chairs of Empire and Regency styles were superseded by deeply buttoned and thickly stuffed padding. This was frequently covered with plush velvet. The invention of wire springs led to easy chairs that had a wooden frame within but no woodwork showing on the outside. They were certainly comfortable, if the shape was right, but some were too 'easy' for long-lasting comfort as they had insufficient firmness to support the body correctly. A plushly upholstered and fairly upright pair of chairs with deep buttoned velvet covering and a characteristic long fringe is illustrated in Plate 63a. A decorative form of rope stool popular in France would have been similarly upholstered, but with no fringe. This stool was of carved wood in the form of a rope knotted at the four toes and at the crossing of the stretchers. Conversation sofas and love seats were also upholstered in this way. They were of two forms: a central round soft sofa with three or four seating places all back to back; and an S-shaped sofa where the two seats were side by side but facing opposite directions.

Two 19th-century wickerwork chairs.

Cheaper and less exotic chairs were also made and supplied for humbler and more practical purposes. Windsor chairs were amongst these and are considered in a separate note. Another form of cheap chair that took on great popularity was that devised by an Austrian, Michael Thonet who faced the demand for mass production by steam bending beechwood to make light chairs. These had a tubular appearance, the woodwork being round in cross section and in a continuous shaped form. He made various sorts of chairs, including rocking chairs, in the same manner. Furniture of this kind is still made and is very popular today.

Another popular form of chair that had developed in England partly out of the Grecian type was the balloon-back chair, not related to the French late eighteenth-century variety. The Victorian balloon-back chair (the term is not a contemporary one) had a totally rounded or horizontal oval back supported on short uprights from the back seat rail and had thin turned tapering legs. It sometimes had a caned seat or otherwise an upholstered-over seat covered with fabric or horse-hair material, which was used on many other chairs, and was popular for its long-lasting strength.

Prie-dieu chairs were very popular in Victorian houses; as well as displaying something of a pious nature they also showed off needle-work done by the ladies.

Papier-mâché furniture was also highly fahionable and was made by firms such as Jennens and Bettridge of Birmingham whose stamp can be seen on many pieces. The framework was entirely made of pulp and this could be decorated in various ways. The most usual was a highly polished black finish superimposed with chinoiserie in gold or with a combination of painting of flowers in natural colours and inlaid pieces of mother-of-pearl. A wide range of chairs were made in this method and were exhibited at the Great Exhibitions of 1851 and 1855 in London and Paris respectively. Balloon- and spoon-back chairs were especially popular. A grandiose version, now in the Victoria and Albert Museum, London, depicts Prince Albert in the back.

Despite the popular trends that grew out of mass production a determined effort was made by some English designers to improve standards of taste and these men had a considerable influence abroad. William Morris (1834–96) led a movement and created a business that emulated aspects of mediaevalism with an emphasis on hand-made objects and art forms that stressed the individuality of handicrafts. Morris turned his back on Georgian proportions and qualities and seemed content to omit the experience and achievements of the eighteenth century in pressing the virtues he advocated. He was also strongly opposed to the use of machinery. His factory supplied

An unusual revolving armchair in maple, probably Russian.

146

chairs that were light, elegant and functional. The 'Sussex' and 'Morris' chairs were made up of plain turned members and are further characterised by a relative complexity of supporting stretchers in parallel pairings and rush seats. The wood was beech, stained or decorated to resemble ebony.

A pair of 19th-century occasional chairs with a fan motif in the back.

Unfortunately, Morris's rejection of machinery and his relatively narrow reference to conventional forms led him and chair design on an artistic tangent from popular requirement. His approach indeed tended to be too specialised and 'arty' and unrelated to the opportunity of developing a general style that with the aid of clever machinery could serve mass production. Further along the tangent the 'Art Furniture' movement of the 1870s and 1880s produced the exotic creations of Burger, Talbert and Eastlake. This in turn was followed by the Aesthetic Movement and the Arts and Crafts Movement. Of

An unusual chair in the form of musical instruments. Probably
English. c. 1900.

A hall porter's leather upholstered chair.

the latter was Ernest Gimson who designed and made a practical type of ladder-back chair, the ladder-back probably partially derived from the ladder-back chairs of the Chippendale period. Both types have a series of parallel flattened rings across the back. Gimson's chair had plain turned spindle legs and stretchers and a rush seat.

The Art Nouveau style was a new temporary style that despite its name originated largely in England. In mood it was basically anti-historical in reaction to the prevalent over-Romanticism of historic revivals. Its forms were based on vegetation and are recognised by strange languid and sinuous curves with leaf and petal motifs. The child's chair and side chair depicted in Plates 63 and 64 illustrate these. C. F. A. Voysey (1857–1941) was an architect and designer much admired on the continent for Art Nouveau styles; he advocated the use of plain oak, totally untreated with colour or polish. The Scottish architect C. R. Mackintosh (1868–1928) enjoyed high repute in his native land and abroad. He designed extraordinary eccentric chairs with very high elongated backs barely ornamented with mysterious shapes and holes. The seat and legs were normal and dull, the seat often of rush and the legs square and tapering. (See PLATE 63)

England was, during the second half of the nineteenth century, a great exporter of furniture to the continent and to many other countries of the world. But this ceased to be the case around the beginning of the present century. The fault partly lay in a mistrust of machinery for making good quality but practical objects in the world of decorative arts. This idea was instigated by William Morris but also felt strongly by later designers. It cost England her supremacy in furniture-making. This passed to Germany where the Werkbund of 1907 and the Bauhaus of 1919 were established, and also to Scandinavia which was ready to produce new lively designs, suitable for fresh modern thinking and living.

These nations have led current trends with inventions that include a cantilever chair of tubular steel made by Marcel Brener in 1925, a laminated birch chair by a Finnish architect, Alvar Aalto in 1929 and a Barcelona chair in stainless steel by Mies van der Rohe. Danish furniture too has proved stylish and popular.

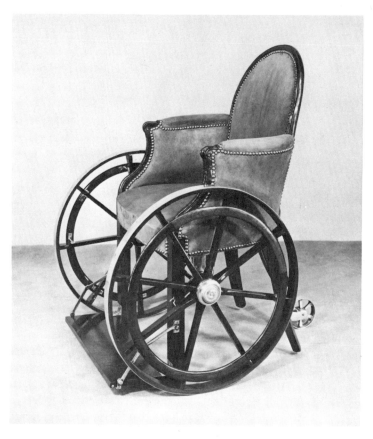

An elegant 19th-century wheel chair modelled around an 18th-century style chair.

But though the field of design remains open, a truly modern style has yet to emerge as a united force and a clear image of the times. Perhaps we, who live in the period, should not be able to see this. I wonder what will be left behind when we have gone for our descendants to remember us by and even treasure perhaps?

7

Windsor Chairs

*I have heard him [Dr Johnson] assert, that
a tavern chair was the throne of human felicity.*

One type of chair that originated in England and was adopted and became even more popular in America, and which has remained little altered, is the Windsor. The origin of its name is a mystery and does not seem to be connected with the fact that many of the type have been supplied to the Royal Household.

In England Windsor chairs have been made in large quantities for humbler domestic use in, for example, cottages, taverns and 'below stairs' servants' quarters in larger houses. In America they have had a more generally respectable use and seem to have particularly suited a less grandiose society. American models were in many respects more sophisticated and graceful than their English counterparts.

The first Windsor chairs emerged in England in the late seventeenth century. These chairs had a fairly high back consisting of spindles or sticks, usually of beech, a solid wood seat slightly scooped out, usually of elm, straight turned legs of beech and a back rail binding the spindles of ash or yew. The earliest type is characterised by a comb-back, which is a top central cresting in the form of a comb, a kind of head-rest extension rising from the spindle back. The hoop-back type became popular around the middle of the eighteenth century. The hoop of the back which held the tops of the spindle sticks was bent by steaming or soaking in water. The other parts of the construction of the chair were equally individual and unrelated to other forms of

A fine Windsor armchair with gothic features. c. 1770.

chair-making. The jointing was not of mortice and tenon as would have been made by joiners, but of the most basic tenon type, the leg ends merely sunk into holes in the bottom of the seat, and the spindles similarly secured. They were the work of turners rather than joiners. Some English Windsor chairs became quite elaborate. They were given cabriole legs, often of a clumsy 'country' shape, and

A yew-wood Windsor armchair with a hoop back.

stretchers between the legs. The middle stretcher was often hoop shaped. A horizontal hoop sometimes made an extra support for the spindle back and extended to the front of the chair on either side in the form of arms. A central splat was from time to time incorporated in the back, and another feature for extra strength was the addition of two bracing spindles behind the middle of the back. Decoration was kept to a minimum on these essentially utility chairs but where a back splat was introduced this might be pierced. Some finer Georgian Windsors have a series of small splats in the back replacing the spindles; these were pierced with Gothic motifs. Occasionally the back was in the form of a pointed Gothic arch. Other models had a wheel or star motif in the back or even Prince of Wales feathers. Some greater houses ordered Windsor chairs of mahogany but these are rare. The original materials and the simplest forms have on the whole prevailed. In some cases the chairs were made entirely of yew except for an elm seat.

A nineteenth-century variant that enjoyed great popularity from about 1830 was the 'smoker's bow', a low backed, stronger chair with thicker turned legs and spindle back. The horizontal back rail and arms were of a hoop shape scrolling out slightly at the arm ends. These tough chairs were used almost universally from kitchens to institutions.

Windsor chairs were always made in quantity. Today they are mass produced in HighWycombe, which has been for a long time a centre of chair-making, but they are now usually made entirely of beech.

American Windsor chairs were from the start more graceful than the English. They fall chiefly into three categories, the low-backed, comb-backed and hoop-backed, and it seems that, unlike in England, they evolved in that order. Also, unlike the English ones, they were made usually of turned maple while the solid seats were of tulip-poplar or pine. They were normally painted, most often a green colour but also red, yellow, black and others. A rocking Windsor chair at the American Museum at Bath is black with gilt 'chinoiseries' showing a very un-Chinese building and a form of wagon. Windsor chairs were more widely used in America than in England and were used in highly respectable as well as informal circumstances. The low-backed armchair made in New York or Philadelphia around the 1770s is most elegant, with fine turned legs, stretchers, arm supports, a thin seat and a light back with thin curved arms. Although many chairs were exported to other parts of the country it appears that they were also made locally and are now hard to distinguish. A low-

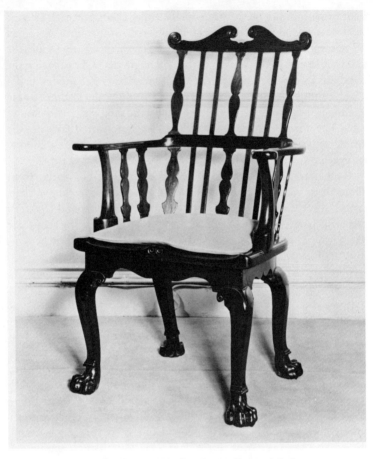

An unusual mahogany Windsor chair with a comb-back top.

backed chair is shown for instance in a Connecticut portrait of *c.* 1775. It has almost identical features to those of New York or Philadelphia and is clearly painted 'bottle' green with the seat scarlet.

The same lightness of style and sophisticated look is reflected in the comb-back chairs. These were often further enhanced with a scroll motif on the ends of the top back rail. The legs remained turned and set into the seat at an angle: the cabriole leg does not seem to have been frequently used on American Windsors.

The final American variety, the hoop-backed chair, was similarly graceful with light spindle-sticks and a flowing back rail curved up from the arms.

Windsor sofas and stools were also made. The sofas, which were sometimes quite long, are a totally American invention. They were not as a rule made in England.

An interesting collection of Windsor chairs and allied variations can be seen at the Henry Francis du Pont Winterthur Museum, Delaware.

8

Construction and Restoration

If I'd as much money as I could spend,
I never would cry old chairs to mend;
Cry chairs to mend, old chairs to mend;
I never would cry old chairs to mend.

The intention of this brief mention of the making and repairing of chairs is to bring to mind a different approach to the study of historical chairs in contrast to the scholastic pursuit of style development. This practical viewpoint can give another dimension to the enjoyment of the pageant of styles.

All but some exceptionally strong chairs or ones that have been placed where they have been little used, have from time to time needed repair in one respect or another. However well-made the piece may be, it is inevitable that joints become dried out and weak and that the frame needs tightening. Sometimes today with a fine example it is decided not to tamper with it and it is put out of practical commission and is museumified, but otherwise most old chairs will need some form of attention every five or ten years. A few people might object in a pious belief that what is antique should not be touched, feeling that the chair should be allowed to deteriorate naturally. This over-zealous attitude can be summarily dismissed since there is no reason why the construction or appearance should be in any way altered in correcting weakness or breakage. In merely preserving the decayed state we can caution ourselves with Pope's condemnation of certain literary critics:

Authors, like coins, grow dear as they grow old;
It is the rust we value, not the gold.

Cautious restoration by knowledgeable and skilful craftsmen is essential and most pieces have been subject to such care over the generations. Standards and styles of repair have of course varied and changed. Today we frequently find iron brackets strengthening old breaks and those we remove so as to get to the weakness in the joint which can usually be glued more satisfactorily. Sometimes it will be necessary to splice-in a piece of wood to give proper support. On other occasions, pieces of carving will have been knocked off or veneers chipped or loosened. These should be replaced or secured to safeguard against further trouble. Gilt and painted furniture has often lost its original lustre but these aspects of patination are not normally altered; they are indeed a true feature of the antiquity, and are preferable in our eyes to the seemingly gaudy tastes of our ancestors. Chips in the surfaces or wounded parts where structural repair has been carried out will naturally be attended to by matching in with the original.

The repair of old chairs is notoriously one of the most difficult tasks of an antique restorer since he frequently has to re-create a sturdy piece from a totally rocking and uneven-footed wreck, without being able to alter the parts which have sometimes become slightly mis-shapen. Hence the plea of the ballad quoted at the head of this note. But on the other hand, the successful repair of a set of chairs can be the most satisfactory experience. Fine pieces almost given up as dead can sometimes be given vital new life by skilful and judicious restoration. However, really good craftsmen are today harder and harder to find. Several men may be needed to restore various aspects of a piece – cabinet-maker or joiner, seat caner, polisher, upholsterer, painter, lacquerer or gilder may be needed. There are many enthusiasts keen to try such skills and a good many bodgers, but not so many experts with the specialist experience needed for first-class restoration.

DESCRIPTION OF THE COLOUR PLATES

Plate 1 – Portrait of Richard II in Westminster Abbey. The King is shown sitting on a mediaeval Gothic-style throne very similar to the chair of the Master of the United Guild of St Mary, and St John and St Catherine at Coventry. The Coventry chair is thought to be the only remaining part of a triple seat that would have been raised on a dais, as were most seats of distinguished rank. Like many French and Spanish mediaeval chests and other furniture the woodwork is elaborately carved with relatively small and intricate tracery within a more general pattern of arches. The large scale and heavy nature of such pieces of furniture indicates that they were not moved much but were essentially a feature of the building in which they were placed. The seat has much in common with the fine choir stalls of the period.

Plate 2 – The gilt throne of the Pharaoh Tutankhamun whose tomb was discovered and excavated by Howard Carter and Lord Carnarvon in 1922. The contents, nearly three and a half thousand years old, include some most beautiful and fascinating furniture. This chair is of wood overlaid with metal, silver and gold, partly enamelled with other colours. The embossed metalwork depicts the boy-king and another figure, with various official and religious motifs and hieroglyphics. The overall form of the chair appears to be timeless and little different from relatively modern models, with similar legs, stretchers and arms. The monopoid lions are especially a feature that is related to modern designs, particularly of the Regency period in England.

Plate 3a – A stool found in the tomb of Tutankhamun. This is of wood decorated and gilt. The legs are in the form of lion's feet and are again similar to some European forms of a much later date, but all the feet face one direction rather than outwards.

Plate 3b – This sofa forms part of a quantity of furniture at Knole, Sevenoaks, Kent, which has survived since the late seventeenth century with its original upholstery and velvet covering. Made with an eye for astonishing plushness and comfort this piece has adjustable wing flaps. English, *c.* 1690.

Plate 4 – A Charles II walnut armchair with a caned back and seat. English, *c.* 1680. This is a typical and fine specimen of a large number of chairs that were made, displaying a richness of pierced carving, often incorporating cherubs and crowns, with turned 'barley sugar' back seat rails, and scroll arms and legs. The crouching lions on the arms of this chair and the crowned mask finials on the back are unusual characteristics.

Plate 5 – An elaborate example of a curious form of chair, commonly referred to as bobbin chairs. They are thought to have a Byzantine origin and to have come to England via an archaic use of the design in Scandinavia. This early seventeenth-century example of ash and oak is entirely made up, with the exception of the flat seat, of 'thrown' or turned pieces worked on a lathe. Less elaborate chairs of the same form were also made and are more common.

Plate 6 – A lovely pair of high-backed William and Mary armchairs decorated with black lacquer with gilt enrichments. The elegant scrolling of the arms and legs, the pierced scrolling carving of the top rails and the front stretchers and the tapering column uprights of the backs, are all features to be noted. The caning of the backs and seats is of the very finely meshed variety that followed the open coarse weave of earlier chairs which preceded the standard weave introduced later and still used today.

Plate 7a – Two finely carved late seventeenth-century stools of walnut with parcel gilding. The arcaded stretchers are decorated with fishes. The interesting legs have a dome-capped acanthus motif and the toes are inward scrolling.

Plate 7b – An early eighteenth-century Queen Anne walnut stool with cabriole legs, the knees being carved with acanthus leaves, parcel gilt, and with a drop-in seat upholstered with contemporary needlework depicting a floral pattern on a yellow ground. English, *c.* 1710.

Plate 8 – Another fine William and Mary walnut stool with boldly turned bulb motif legs and stretchers. The stool is upholstered with needlework of the period.

Plate 9a – A William and Mary walnut stool with crossed stretchers with a central finial echoing the bulb turnings on the legs.

Plate 9b – A Queen Anne or George I walnut stool with parcel gilding on the knees. The legs are carved with an unusual dog-mask motif and terminate in claw and ball feet. The seat is upholstered with early eighteenth-century needlework.

Plate 10a – A Dutch settee and an armchair of the first quarter of the eighteenth century. Both are of walnut with splats inlaid with various woods and have carved shell motifs on the seat rails and back rails. Both have 'shepherd crook' arms but the settee has ball and claw feet while the chair has scroll toes carved with an acanthus leaf.

Plate 10b – This pair of William and Mary red lacquer side chairs show elements of transition towards the simpler graceful lines of the Queen Anne period. The top rails are still decorated with elaborate carving and include a shell motif but the legs are of plainer cabriole form, joined by stretchers. The back of the chair is splayed out slightly and is carved at the top and has a central splat. On later chairs the cane-work was omitted.

Plate 11a – A pair of Queen Anne walnut side chairs with cabriole legs in the front and plainer legs at the back with stretchers joining the four legs for added strength. The chairs are entirely upholstered from the seat upwards and covered with needlework, not the original.

Plate 11b – A pair of graceful Queen Anne walnut side chairs of a similar form but with cabriole legs in front and at the back. In this later form there is no stretcher at all. The legs terminate in simple pad feet. The backs are again totally upholstered.

Plate 12 – One of a pair of early eighteenth-century cream lacquer side chairs with decoration in other colours. The rounded back, which has a carved cresting, is caned and has a central splat. The legs are carved on the knees and joined by stretchers with a finial in the centre.

Plate 13 – An eighteenth-century Dutch side chair decorated with black and gold japanning and with an upholstered-over seat. The curvilinear back has a central splat shaped to support the back, *c.* 1745.

Plate 14 – A fine Queen Anne walnut armchair of a popular form that had a solid curved back and shaped open arms. The knees are carved with a characteristic plain line motif and the legs terminate in pad feet. The upholstered-over seat is covered with fine needlework.

Plate 15 – A similar armchair of slightly later date. This one has shepherd's crook arms, the ends of the arms being somewhat looped. The legs are carved with a shell motif on the knees and with claw and ball feet. The seat of this chair is upholstered on a 'drop-in' frame and again is covered with fine needlework.

Plate 16 – An early eighteenth-century walnut library, reading or cock-fighting chair with its original leather upholstery and with a flap on the back which would support a book if one sat on the chair back to front.

Plate 17 – An oval Queen Anne walnut stool with cabriole legs. The inside of the tops of the legs have a simple scroll moulding and the legs terminate in the classic pad feet of the period. The stool has a drop-in seat upholstered with needlework.

Plates 18 and 19 – An armchair and a single chair of a set attributed to the early eighteenth-century furniture maker, Giles Grendy. These chairs are of red lacquer with gilt chinoiserie decoration. The cabriole legs are joined by stretchers. The uprights are elegantly shaped and the central splats are also beautifully shaped with scrolling motifs. The seats are caned.

Plate 20 – A very fine imposing gilt chair of the early eighteenth century, formerly at Benningborough Hall, Yorkshire. Of carved wood and gesso, it is profusely decorated on the background with a stamped ring pattern.

Plate 21 – A magnificent giltwood and gesso side chair. English *c*. 1720. The beautiful flowing lines of the framework are the chair's chief quality, but this is further enriched with restrained carving as on the knees, toes and the heraldic crest on the top of the chair. A similar chair, probably from the same set, upholstered in red and gold cut velvet, is in the Victoria and Albert Museum, London.

Plate 22 – A fine curvilinear backed walnut side chair of the reign of George I. These chairs are differentiated from Queen Anne chairs by rather more carved ornament. This consists of the inverted shell on the top of the splat, the leaf motifs where the splat is joined to the uprights, the shells on the knees, the claw and ball feet and the other smaller motifs. The drop-in seat is covered in contemporary needlework.

Plate 23 – Another fine chair of the same period. This has the more elaborate ornament of the 1720s but also features of earlier chairs. The straight top rail and the stretchers joining the legs are a latent aspect of design. Again the seat is of the 'drop-in' variety and covered with needlework.

Plate 24a – An early eighteenth-century gilt and carved gesso sofa with cabriole legs and outward scrolling arms. The upholstered back is framed by a light filet of woodwork contributing to an overall gracefulness.

Plate 24b – A good pair of mid-eighteenth-century English armchairs of carved beechwood and gilded. It can clearly be seen in this example how fashions in England followed the French, but nevertheless, were tempered with more restraint. English, *c.* 1770.

Plate 25 – A fine quality carved gilt gesso early eighteenth-century wing chair upholstered with modern velvet. The gesso legs are all of a highly sophisticated broken cabriole form, finely carved and stamped. This chair, as the walnut wing chair, has outward scrolling flat arms.

Plate 26 – A fine George I walnut wing chair upholstered with good original needlework. On the better wing chairs the back legs are also cabriole in form. Others have plain straight legs set at a slight angle.

Plate 27 – A magnificent eighteenth-century giltwood rococo armchair, *c.* 1740. The arms, apron around the seat frame and the legs are delicately carved with foliate patterns. The front toes are outward scrolling. The chair is upholstered with tapestry.

Plate 28 – A fine mid-eighteenth-century Italian armchair painted in blue with gold decoration. In style this chair shows French Louis XV influence but an especially Italian feature is the large wide back, particularly broad at the top.

Plate 29 – A very fine Chippendale period rococo armchair of the middle of the eighteenth century. Of beechwood this is exuberantly carved in furious frolicking scrolls and gilded. The arms are especially vital. The legs and back are more controlled; the back is carved with a gadrooned moulding.

Plate 30 – A giltwood armchair of the same type but earlier in feeling. In this case the arm supports and legs only show, apart from a very slender beaded moulding around the seat frame. The elaborate carving is shown on a background of fish scales. The chair has the hump-shaped back top rail that was an elegant feature of the mid-eighteenth century.

Plate 31 – A magnificently carved mahogany Gainsborough armchair formerly at St Giles, Dorset, a house where Chippendale worked. The feet are in the Chinese taste as is some of the fretwork on the legs but the rest of the carving depicts natural leaves, berries, etc.

Plate 32 – A fine Chippendale mahogany armchair in the Chinese taste with trellis back and pierced fret brackets supporting the seat and legs. The top rail is carved with a family crest in the centre and the seat is rounded, a fashion that was fairly common during the second half of the eighteenth century.

Plate 33 – One of a set of Chippendale mahogany chairs with slender show-wood frames around the upholstered back. The chairs are largely derived from the French taste, with delicate cabriole legs and scrolling toes.

Plate 34 – A Chinese Chippendale mahogany side chair upholstered with fine needlework on a dark background. The straight chinoiserie legs are carved with blind fretwork, in the Chinese manner.

Plate 35 – One of a set of mahogany Gainsborough armchairs made by James Gordon. The dark mahogany is crisply carved with fish scales. The chair has a beautifully shaped seat rail, and cabriole legs at front and back.

Plate 36 – One of a magnificent pair of eighteenth-century Indian ivory armchairs with caned seats. The design is of European origin but the chairs also have many native features. The ivory is exquisitely carved with an especially fine pierced back splat and side panels, in the form of intertwined palm leaves. The chairs have five legs joined by a stretcher and terminating in elegant claw and ball feet. The arms terminate in serpents' heads. The ivory is overall finely carved and en-

graved and some of the details are picked out in gold. There is a sofa
en suite.

Plate 37a – A pair of late eighteenth-century Italian gilt-wood
armchairs, elaborately carved in the neo-classical tradition, with
wing-shaped arms ending in scrolled acanthus leaves, the front seat
rails being concave shaped and carved with fluting, and the front legs
being round, tapering and reeded. The chairs bear an indistinct trade
label which indicates that they were made in Lucca, *c.* 1780.

Plate 37b – A pair of fine late eighteenth-century Italian side chairs,
Piedmontese, *c.* 1770. Of neo-classical form these have an elegance and
refinement of style more typical of English than Italian furniture of
the period. The somewhat filigree carved decoration is finely exe-
cuted and was originally entirely gilt but the gilding is now beautifully
worn. The most unusual outward curving legs anticipate the Empire
imitations of classical forms. Modern velvet upholstery.

Plates 38/39 – A fine pair of English armchairs of beechwood
and gilt made in the French taste. These chairs were made for
Harewood House, Yorkshire, where Chippendale was employed.
The lines of these however have no suggestion of Chippendale's
hand. The proportions are very fine and the woodwork is lightly
carved, with gadrooning and other moulding patterns. The fine
needlework is of a later date.

Plate 40 – An Italian neo-classical painted grey armchair, the legs
and arms with a spiral turned pattern. Again we note the wide back of
the chair, an Italian characteristic, and the light show-wood frame of
the back. The seat rails are slightly serpentine shaped at the front of the
chair.

Plate 41 – A fine mahogany armchair in the French taste of the
later part of the eighteenth century, with elegant cabriole legs ending
in scroll toes. The back, seat rail and legs are edged with delightful
gadroon moulding. The elegant lines and proportions of the chair
gives it something of a dancing appearance.

Plates 42/43 – A pair of Adam giltwood armchairs and a small foot
stool en suite, *c.* 1780. The neo-classical legs are round tapering and
fluted and end in elongated small ball feet. At the tops of the legs can
be seen the formal rosettes or paterae which is a hallmark of neo-

classicism. The small oval backs of the chairs are wholly upholstered.

Plate 44 – A fine late eighteenth-century Adam-period painted armchair in blue and white. This chair shows elements of French transitional design: the small oval back being a legacy of the Louis XV preference and the neo-classical legs and other carved decoration being a feature of Louis XVI chairs. The back arms and seat rails have a moulding of stylised husks, a popular neo-classical motif.

Plate 45 – One of a fine pair of Sheraton mahogany shield-back armchairs with large boldly carved Prince of Wales feathers, bound by a coronet in the back. The delicately drawn arms and square tapering front legs are simple and graceful, all the emphasis of the design being focused on the motif in the backs, *c.* 1775.

Plates 46/47 – Part of a set of seat furniture of turned and carved beechwood simulating bamboo. Furniture in the Chinese taste had been popular since the seventeenth century but this form evolved about 1770. The chair shapes are essentially those of the Chippendale period, with trellis backs, curved seats, slightly humped top rails, bracket supports under the seats and stretchers between the legs. The furniture is decorated with red lacquer with gilt chinoiserie decoration.

Plates 48/49 – A set of four walnut Louis XV fauteuils or armchairs, *c.* 1760. Beech was the more usual wood and was often painted or gilt. These chairs have a lightness and elegance that was admired and imitated all over Europe.

Plate 50a – A pair of small Louis XVI side chairs of beechwood with traces of original painting. The round arched backs are derived from a balloon shape commemorating early flights in a balloon. The chairs have round, fluted, tapering legs and the splats are interesting with spindles resting on large roundels and splayed out at the top.

Plate 50b – Two of a set of giltwood arm and side chairs, probably English, *c.* 1780 but closely associated with Louis XVI models. They have curved square backs, padded arms, rounded seats and round tapering legs with square tops decorated with paterae.

Plate 51a – One of a large set of armchairs in the manner of James Wyatt, an architect designer in the Adam tradition who favoured simpler lines with less conspicuous decoration of a filigree nature. The chairs have shield backs and square tapering legs. The woodwork is decorated with husks, beadwork and paterae in carton-pierre, a composition material. This is gilded in contrast to the white painted woodwork.

Plate 51b – Two chairs of a set of giltwood chairs and sofas supplied for Northumberland House and probably designed by Robert Adam. In the Louis XVI manner the chair has a square back with a slightly arched top rail, finely carved back surround, and typical neoclassical arm supports and legs, in the form of bulbous reeded columns, c. 1780.

Plate 52 – An unusual and rare late eighteenth-century Indian solid ivory armchair with a carved back and seat. The spindles in the back, around the seat rail, and the arm supports and front legs all turned with oriental bulb shapes. The top rail is finely pierced and carved and is capped with three small finials.

Plate 53 – A fine late eighteenth-century mahogany tub chair with finely carved and shaped arm fronts, a flowing, curved seat rail, and carved and fluted front legs. This is the equivalent of the French bergère which offered great comfort for reading. Note the curious straight back leg which extends out of the hidden back of the chair at an acute angle.

Plate 54a – A pair of giltwood armchairs with elegant rococo lines, oval backs, cabriole legs and finely curved arm supports. The carved decoration, however, is neo-classical with fluting along the seat rails and a central patera overhung with a swag of husks. There are further swags on the front knees.

Plate 54b – A pair of Russian mahogany side chairs of the late eighteenth century. This simple and elegant model is partly in-spired by Louis XVI styles and is neo-classical in spirit, with an em-phasis of straight lines. These are accentuated by the overlaid brass-work which is in long ribbed pieces, highly polished. There are brass roundels at the corners of the back and seat frame.

Plate 55a – A magnificent pair of Adam period giltwood armchairs in which elements of rococo design are happily merged with the later fashionable neo-classicism. The chairs have large round backs and seats of an ample size. The arm supports and legs are gracefully curved and the toes are scrolled. The seat rails are fluted and on the points a small apron motif hangs down with foliate carving, *c*. 1770.

Plate 55b – A fine pair of late eighteenth-century armchairs in the form of Louis XV bergères. While the shape is essentially French, the neo-classical decoration is typically English in manner.

Plate 56 – A fine late eighteenth-century armchair of the Adam period, with restrained neo-classical decorative carved motifs. The chair is upholstered with tapestry seat, back and arm-pads.

Plate 57 – An attractive painted side chair of the end of the eighteenth century. The beechwood frame is delicately painted with blue and white neo-classical decoration. The chair has a caned seat. Probably originally made for a bedroom or a passage.

Plate 58a – A pair of Regency tub chairs probably designed by George Smith, but with elements also familiar of designs by Thomas Hope. The mahogany frames are dominated by the powerful monopoid lions that form the front legs. A carved wreath pattern runs around the seats, *c*. 1810. A chair with similar lion masks and with the same stylised mane is in the Royal Collection at Buckingham Palace.

Plate 58b – A pair of William IV armchairs decorated in maroon lacquer with gilt chinoiseries, possibly oriental. The balloon shaped backs are composed of graceful scrolls while the thicker turned front legs reflect a certain coarsening of style. The chairs have caned seats and velvet cushions, *c*. 1835.

Plate 59 – A fine Sheraton painted armchair with shield back and turned front legs. The beechwood frame is painted black and on this background motifs in pink and other colours include hanging drapery.

Plate 60 – An unusual English Regency armchair, *c*. 1815, the woodwork and decoration with elaborate semi-Greek–Etruscan motifs. The lines of the woodwork are noticeably geometrical, a feature of some forms of neo-classicism. In this case circles, straight lines and angles are emphasised. The chair is painted and gilded, the latter superimposed with key pattern decoration.

Plate 61 – An early nineteenth-century X-frame carved giltwood armchair the front and back uprights in the form of strange birds whose wings frame the seat rails. The legs of the chair are hairy animals' legs with claw feet. Probably German or Italian, possibly English.

Plate 62 – An interesting side chair designed by Bugatti of various woods overlaid with embossed brasswork and inlaid with metals. The back and seat of the chair are of painted leather. The chair is of a consciously eclectic design, combining a Middle Eastern flavour with Art Nouveau aspects. The attractively curved back is inlaid with brass and pewter butterflies, and the seat is supported by quadruple cluster columns standing on circular disc legs, *c.* 1900.

Plate 63a – A comfortable pair of English soft upholstered side chairs, *c.* 1840, with deep buttoned red velvet and a long fringe around the seat.

Plate 63b – An Art Nouveau red lacquer side chair with a tall narrow back carved with long iris leaves and flowers, the solid stretcher, seat and legs similarly decorated. English, *c.* 1890.

Plate 63c – A chair designed by C. R. Mackintosh (1868–1928) of oak stained with a dark polish and with an upholstered drop-in seat. This chair was exhibited at the Vienna Secession Exhibition in 1900. The square tapering legs are reminiscent of late eighteenth-century chairs, but the elongated back and oval at the top are original.

Plate 64 – An Art Nouveau painted child's chair, the woodwork of vegetable-like languid forms. The legs are not at the corners but on the four sides and there is a solitary stretcher from front to back. The needlework cushion is a later addition.

Bibliography

World Furniture, edited by Helena Hayward, Hamlyn, 1965.

The Dictionary of English Furniture, Percy Macquoid and Ralph Edwards, Country Life, Second Edition, 1954.

A History of English Furniture, Percy Macquoid, Caxton.

The Country Life Book of Chairs, Edward T. Joy, Country Life Books, 1967.

Windsor Chairs, F. Gordon Roe, Phoenix House, 1953.

English Chairs, Introduction by Ralph Edwards, Victoria and Albert Museum, H.M.S.O., 1970.

Furniture 700–1700, Eric Mercer, Weidenfeld & Nicolson, 1969.

Three Centuries of Furniture in Colour, H. D. Molesworth and John Kenworthy-Brown, Michael Joseph, 1972.

A Book of American Furniture, Doreen Beck, Hamlyn, 1973.

Great Houses, Nigel Nicolson, Weidenfeld & Nicolson, 1968.

Great Houses of Britain, Nigel Nicolson, Spring Books, 1968.

Great Interiors, edited by Ian Grant, Weidenfeld & Nicolson, 1967.

Great Palaces, Sacheverell Sitwell et al., Hamlyn, 1969.

Great Houses of Europe, edited by Sacheverell Sitwell, Spring Books, 1961.

Buckingham Palace, John Harris, John Russell, Geoffrey de Bellaigne, Oliver Millar, Nelson, 1968.

The Victorian Country House, Mark Girouard, Oxford University Press, 1971.

Glossary

Amorini (Italian) Infant cupid figures of a sculptural decorative nature.

Anthemion Of Greek origin, a stylised honeysuckle pattern, associated with neo-classicism.

Arabesque Intertwined foliage and stylised figures as patterned ornament.

Art Nouveau Style born in England in 1880s and developed in Europe. Uses languid plant-like decorative motifs.

Baluster A turned column of various shapes, used in legs, backs and arm supports of chairs.

Baroque Style evolved in seventeenth century with characteristic florid decoration associated with movement, sculptural forms and bright colours.

Bentwood Wood steamed into carved shapes, especially as used by Thonet for chairs and other furniture.

Bevel A slant or inclination on a surface as often found at the edge of a mirror plate, or panels of wood.

Blind Fret Fret carving in bas-relief so that the surface is not pierced. Associated with Chinese motifs and the Chippendale period.

Bombé (French) A swelling or bulge on the sides or fronts of commodes especially, but also reflected in other furniture.

Boulle A technique of marquetry decoration chiefly of brass and tortoiseshell perfected by André Charles Boulle in France during the reign of Louis XIV.

Burr A specially contorted, gnarled figuring with a lively texture in wood where it has grown as a wart-like excrescence on a tree. Burr walnut, burr yew and burr elm were especially used.

Cabriole Leg A nineteenth-century term for a type of curved leg as perfected in eighteenth-century France and England. Originally based on an animal's leg (carved with hair, hoof, paw and claw, etc.). The word, derived from French and Italian sources connected with dancing and animal movements.

Cane Strips of natural fibre imported for weaving chair seats and backs, at first used coarsely with a wide mesh, then very finely (late seventeenth century), and subsequently to a standard medium.

Cartouche Baroque decorative plaque usually carved wood or metal, sometimes used as central finial in pediment or cresting, and on chairs as a carved bas-relief motif on knees, etc.

Chinoiserie European imitation of oriental decoration, especially of lacquer: coloured and gilt Chinese motifs on a red, white, black, green, blue or tortoiseshell background.

Ciseleurs (French) Carvers and chasers of ormolu mounts.

Colour Specifically, the natural tones of wood and as developed as a result of polishing and age.

Console Scroll-shaped bracket and more particularly a type of side table often made to go under a pier-glass based on this form.

Coromandel A wood otherwise known as calamander. Also Chinese lacquer with incised decoration, chiefly late seventeenth century, and occasionally used on chairs.

Cresting The top decorative piece on a cabinet clock or chair sometimes of a contrasting material such as carved giltwood.

Crossbanding A surface veneer edging, the grain being at right angles to the main part of the surface.

Curule A style of chair of French late eighteenth-century origin where the legs are of X-form across the front and back.

Dovetail A shaped slot-in joint in woodwork.

Dowel An internal peg in a joint in woodwork.

Ebeniste (French) Cabinetmaker.

Ebonised Polished to a shiny black colour simulating ebony.

Figuring The natural grain patterns in wood, featured in solid wood but especially in selected veneers.

Finial An urn-shaped motif often used on the top of clock-cases, cabinets, chair-back uprights, stretcher crossings, etc.

Flute, Fluting Parallel grooves as in classical columns. Stop fluting is when these grooves are partially filled around the base of the column.

Gadrooning A decorative moulding consisting of tear shaped lobs linked side by side.

Gesso A composition of gypsum used for preparing surfaces for gilding, sometimes elaborately carved before gilding.

Grisaille Painted decoration in tones of grey.

Intarsia (Italian) Marquetry as used in the Renaissance and after, in wood and stone.

Japanning European imitation of oriental lacquer. See Chinoiserie.

Linenfold A modern term describing a conventional carved pattern in wood panelling resembling loosely pleated material. Seen on panels on early oak chairs.

Marquetry Contrasting veneers and other materials including tortoiseshell inlaid in surfaces representing scenes, floral decoration, etc.

Mortise & Tenon Concealed cavity and tongue respectively, in woodwork joint.

Ogee Flattened S-shaped moulding pattern, plane surface in serpentine form.

Ormolu Furniture mounts and objects of cast bronze, chased and gilded.

Papier-Maché Paper pulp used like composition material as substitute for wooden frames in chairs, etc.

Parcel Gilt Partly gilt. Carved decoration and mouldings are sometimes picked out in gold to contrast with polished wood surfaces.

Parquetry Veneers or solid wood laid in contrasting geometric patterns.

Patera Classical rosette or oval used for decoration, a feature of neo-classicism. Plural: paterae.

Penwork Black decoration on natural coloured wood of a satinwood or pale colour.

176

Pierced Fret carving often of a Chinese inspired trellis pattern.

Pilaster A flattened architectural column, a feature of early Georgian as well as neo-classical furniture.

Putti Naked cupid figures similar to amorini. See Amorini.

Repoussé An elaborate embossed pattern in metalwork, where the decoration is hammered out from behind.

Rococo Asymmetric florid patterns, derived from shellwork, and the basis of mid-eighteenth-century style.

Romanesque Eleventh- and twelfth-century style characterised by plain rounded arches, with superficial decoration.

Sabre Leg A backward curving leg resembling a sabre sword; concave.

Serpentine A curved form, resembling the windings of a snake.

Single Chair A side chair, one without arms.

Splat The vertical centre panel in the backs of chairs.

Strapwork Ornament, largely Tudor, of intertwined banding, also seen on gesso furniture.

Stretcher Joining cross-bar between legs on tables and chairs.

Stringing Line(s) of inlay, usually boxwood or ebony.

Swag(s) Garlands of foliage, flowers or husks either in bas-relief or wholly sculptural.

Term A caryatid figure as a support with a pedestal base below and the top half of the human form.

Thrown Applied to woodwork that is turned on a lathe. See Turned.

Trompe-L'œil Painting or marquetry done in a realistic perspective manner to deceive the eye into believing it reality.

Turned Wood or other material shaped on a lathe, as in spindle, bobbin or baluster forms.

Veneer Thin cut sheets of wood chosen for its fine qualities of colour, figuring and texture, used for covering frame and carcase surfaces.

Vitruvian Scroll Wave-like or vertical continuous C-scroll pattern of classical origin, much used by William Kent and the neo-classicists.

Index

Figures in italics refer to the page numbers of illustrations in the text, those in bold type are plate numbers.